# My Last Summer as a Fat Girl

My Last Summer as a Fat Girl

Dr. Ellie Henkind Katz

Copyright © 2017 by Dr. Ellie Henkind Katz www.elliekatz.com

Cover Design:

All rights reserved. No part of this publication may be reproduced, distributed, or transmitted in any form or by any means, including photocopying, recording, or other electronic or mechanical methods, without the prior written permission of the publisher, except in the case of brief quotations embodied in critical reviews and certain other noncommercial uses permitted by copyright law.

# My Last Summer as a Fat Girl

*Dr. Ellie Henkind Katz*

# Introduction

*July 20ᵗʰ*

I feel an urgency to write while the taste of hazelnuts, chocolate chips and cookie dough still lingers in my mouth. I am experiencing a change in my breathing and heart rate, a sense of impending euphoria. But after the elation, sated to the point of nausea, I know there will be the inevitable tumble. Tumble and drop are euphemisms for the plummet, the death-defying dive from the high board into a little bucket of water: in other words, defeat.

I have done it again. I have murdered myself in cold blood. I have turned into a raging bull. Nothing is safe in my path. After the rampage, I have become intensely fragile.

I was sure I was finished with this nonsense by now. For such a long time, I've been meticulous with my food and my honesty. I thought I was learning to deal with my emotions and then I go and do a thing like this.

\* \* \*

Before writing these words, I had just watched a TV report on human trafficking that left me so disheartened, I wolfed down four breathtakingly delicious, oversized hazelnut/chocolate chip cookies.

What's the link between cookie consumption and current events?

It's just what I do when I'm overwhelmed. Thank God I am not a drug addict.

Before we go back to the beginning of that year, let me introduce myself. My patients call me Dr. Ellie; my friends call me Elle. To a large crowd of admiring grandchildren, I am Gwammy.

I have been working in the field of psychology for forty years. Initially, my interest was in psycho-linguistics and nonverbal communication, but I found that my true calling was linked to what I could do for humanity. I switched my orientation toward the clinical when I was pregnant with my fourth child, over three decades ago. I have worked with addicts of all sizes and shapes and with addictions that range from heroin and gambling to phobias and codependency.

I have always had a love-hate relationship with food; we go back a long time, food and I. Last year, I decided to master my food intake once and for all. Since people tend to show more of themselves in the summer when they're scantily clad, I thought the idea of a summer to summer sounded just right for me.

While the experiment failed to produce *all* the results I had hoped for, it did bring me–or at least, started to bring me–to a much deeper place in my spiritual evolution.

Though I began with the clear goal of losing weight, I found many more treasures along the way.

I offer this book as an entertaining yet thought-provoking adventure. You are invited to go on the journey with me. I hope that something in these pages may hoist your spirits and inspire you.

I'd like to open with a short preface that explains a little of my background. It is a fragment of the historical Ellie, a glimpse into the origins of my romance with food.

# The Early Years

When I look at photographs from my childhood, I see two distinct phases of myself. One is perfectly reasonably-sized little girl, anywhere up to the age of five, with crossed eyes and a smile. She seems cheerful and lively. In some photos, she romps around with friends, looking quite playful. She is pictured in different seasons, sometimes in a snowsuit, sometimes in a bathing suit. She runs, jumps and even climbs a tree. Always with a smile.

The other little girl is a five-to-ten-year-old monstrosity. She is shockingly larger than her peers, oddly dressed, ungainly. The spark is missing.

There is a picture of me sitting in a bathtub. I am about eight. I am nude. All I'm wearing is a rubber bathing cap, which is placed on top of my head. I have obviously not mastered the cap, because my long hair is cascading down my shoulders and the strap is dangling, unfastened. Why was I even wearing a bathing cap in the tub?

The rolls of fat are pronounced. I look ridiculous. I have no idea who took the picture. What were they thinking?

There is an obvious presence of bosoms; you might stake your claim that they are part of the fat continuum, but I don't think so. I definitely do not look like a fat boy.

I wear a peculiar smile on my face. It's not coquettish but more embarrassed, as if I know I look weird but can't challenge the photographer. Again, I need to ask: Who, in God's name, would want to immortalize me in that pose? And it surely was a pose, as I was smiling for the camera, clearly trying to please someone.

There are other pictures, real looloos, like the one taken when I played Henny Penny in the school production of *Chicken Little*. Wow, I look amazing. I'm in the lineup with the rest of the cast. We're all second graders, but I look like the teacher's aide. I've got double chins all the way down to my knees. For some inexplicable reason, I'm in shorts. Whose idea was that? Maybe Miss Lipshitz, our teacher, pictured in the background with a corsage. She was proud of us.

To this day, I still remember my part: standing there, stiff as a tree trunk, my legs slightly spread apart to steady my nerves. Terrified, I sang, "The sky is going to fall." Funny I was given such a prophetic role.

\* \* \*

When I was born, breastfeeding wasn't popular in New York. It was considered something that backward women would do. It never occurred to my mother to nurse me. I can't fault her for it.

My mom had a pediatrician with an interesting theory of nutrition for newborns. According to this doctor, I was to drink only formula for the first year of my life. I absolutely never chewed anything! My mother went along with this. Imagine that I, the great food-lover, never got a taste of anything besides milk formula until I was a full year old. It boggles my mind.

Years ago, my mom told me that between the ages of four and five, I did not gain an ounce. From what I gather, my caretakers were in a panic and shoved anything and everything down my throat in order for me to gain weight and grow properly. I can't imagine how threatened I must have felt. This hysteria about weight gain must have sent me weird messages about food because from the age of five, I was hooked on eating.

* * *

I have almost no memories before five, except of my eye patch, which used to dig into my face. The clumsy plastic contraption was mean against my skin. My hair, something I didn't manage well, was forever getting tangled in the elastic band that held the patch in place.

We made yearly visits to the eye doctor. I can still remember squirming when the horse-toothed ophthalmologist peered into my eyes at close range. I had no pain in my eyes and did not know what all the fuss was about. I did not comprehend this patch business.

Understand, please, that I did not know I was cross-eyed.

I was not remotely prepared for what was to follow. The only time I'd heard the word "operation" was in reference to our neighbor, Joey. He was born with some serious medical challenges. *He* had operations.

It's possible that I thought the operation would make

me look like him. In my limited cognition, the logical consequence of an operation was to become like Joey. I knew enough of life to realize he looked different. I adored him, but I was not interested in being like him.

With this in my mind, I faced my surgery. I still remember the smell of the ether. When they placed the mask on me, I heard voices droning in the background and felt myself spinning in a tunnel.

I woke up in the recovery room, absolutely without sight. For all I knew, I would never see again. Both eyes were surgically repaired simultaneously, leaving me bandaged and in the dark.

No one prepared me at all for this operation and its recovery period. I had no concept of temporary or permanent. Being only five years old, those days swathed in bandages were my forever.

This must have been an unnerving dance with trauma. While I do not distinctly remember all of my feelings at the time, I have an emotional, tactile memory of fumbling and screaming in terror. The scream went on in my head long after the bandages came off.

According to my mother of blessed memory, when I got my eyes back, the following things occurred: I began to make up stories, a euphemism for lies and gross distortions of the truth; I took up the freaky habit of pulling the eyes out of all my dolls; and I acquired an insatiable hunger.

I still wonder what I did to the dolls whose eyes were merely painted on.

\* \* \*

I developed very, very early after that. I have tried, for a long time, to come up with a theory to explain my ridiculous growth spurt. I went from being an absolutely normal-sized, even slim and lithe little girl to a monstrosity. I was appreciably taller and heavier than the boys and girls three or four grades above me. No one believed me when I told them my age.

My large bulk did not prevent me from being forced to attend dancing lessons. A few times a week, I had to go and prance around in Miss Gracie's basement studio. I liked the dance attire; I loved my ballet shoes, my toe shoes, my tap shoes, the leotards and the tights. It was when I was forced to wear the tutu that I wanted to die. Year after year in our performances, I waddled out, a laughingstock. I looked like a sugar plum fairy about to explode.

\*\*\*

My brother had his Bar Mitzvah when I was eight. That was the winter of third grade, when I was not much smaller than the thirteen-year-old girls whom my brother invited to attend the gala event. I was a little less grotesque, however, than in first and second grade; as my height picked up, my weight was more evenly distributed.

In the spring that followed, we went on a family vacation to Bermuda. Remember, I was only eight years old. For a reason I cannot possibly fathom, I was at one point alone, on my own in the hotel, learning to play ping pong. My instructor was a college student playing in the band to make a few extra bucks during spring break.

Somehow, he invited me to visit his room–I remember

the bed, the night table and the lamp. I remember being forced to touch him. There is a gap, dark and vicious, that separates me today from what other things happened there.

What I do know is that when I escaped and found my way back to my brother and parents, I told them plenty. My brother and father were wild. I remember the scene vividly, my mother trying to stop them from doing anything rash in retaliation.

I knew nothing much about life, let alone the birds and the bees. I was a large-for-my-age, friendly and intelligent eight-year-old. In those days, children were rarely exposed to anything "inappropriate," at least not in my world. Imagine my surprise when my ping pong teacher violated me. I know, of course, that I was sexually abused. I prefer to honor the fact that I don't remember too much. It feels better this way. Trust me.

The matter was never discussed. My trauma was never addressed therapeutically and I conveniently managed to bury the whole event until a family vacation almost thirty years later, when I was pregnant with my fourth child.

The baby *in utero* was particularly restless as I sat down to meditate. The three other kids were at the hotel pool and I was alone in the room with this rumbling in my womb. All of a sudden, I flashed back to that spring break in Bermuda.

My memories were fuzzy, but I accessed his room, and him sitting on the edge of the bed, exposed. It was then that I understood why I always felt so queasy in hotels. It was a gigantic insight. It explained so many years of an unclear, pervasive tension around vacations.

I finally got around to asking my parents and my

brother about Bermuda. They all confirmed that something horrible had occurred but declined to go into detail. They opted to spare me.

As a psychologist and family therapist who has worked for decades with all kinds of afflictions, I have come to understand that those who struggle with eating disorders tend to have murky sexual histories. Whatever transpired in that hotel room, it reinforced a lifetime of eating to drown out the shame.

\*\*\*

In the summer after fourth grade, I was sent to camp. It was my fourth summer away from home. I have my own opinions about farming out little kids so early in their lives, but I won't dwell on that now.

When I came back, to my surprise, my parents and brother were neatly situated in a new house, in a new town. As I look back on this in retrospect, it was logical for them to get me out of their hair so they could move.

For me, it was indescribably traumatic. I simply left the old house one day to go to camp and never returned to it.

\*\*\*

One of the kids in the old neighborhood taught me my first dirty word: shit. It was exciting to add it to my vocabulary. *Shit* sounded so daring and direct. I was overjoyed with the new word, even though I was warned not to say it in public.

## The Early Years

One fine day, I took a piece of colored chalk—green, I think—and printed, in my best hand, those four letters on the street in front of our house. Someone snitched on me and my mom came running out to see with her own eyes what her misfit of a daughter had done.

I got yanked into the house by my ear. It was a first and last act of physical violence. She made me open wide, thrusting a bar of soap into my mouth. I was sent to my room to think about my scandalous behavior.

After a cooling-off period, I snuck down to the basement and hoisted myself up into one of the creepy closets in the boiler room. It was built into the wall. I had to climb on a chair to get in.

It was my first time ever opening one of them, as the boiler room was quite off-limits. I was scared to death, but single-minded. The light was broken so I couldn't even see what was in the closet. I remember pungent paint smells and maybe turpentine.

For what I had done, for the shame I had caused my family, I knew I didn't deserve better than that. Let the punishment fit the crime. The soap was way too mild.

Self-inflicted punishment began here.

\*\*\*

The first time I opened our old freezer in the new house, I got an electric shock. It was one of those shocks you see in a cartoon; it sure scared the hell out of me.

For the next six or seven years, I snuck into the freezer wearing thick rubber gloves. I enlisted the aid of a broom handle to create a lever to pry open the hinge. I knew what treasures awaited me in that freezer. My mom hid food down there, figuring it was safe because I was afraid of the famous shock. In those years, I developed a taste for frozen cookies. I also taught myself how to eat quickly while standing up.

The only housework my mom ever did was to bake desserts for our elegant Sabbath meals. For several days a week, the cookies and cakes were on display in the dining room. She kept them under lock and key, but I always found the key. It was a game of cat and mouse. One of the sickest, cleverest con jobs I ever pulled was when I came downstairs on tiptoe to have my way with some angel food cake. I sliced off a huge wedge, which I cut in half. I cringe to tell this, but I put one half in my bra, held the other slice in my hand and made a lot of noise on purpose. It was midnight and all was quiet in the house. My parents came downstairs, caught me red-handed and ordered me to put the cake back. Little did they know that I had a good-sized portion waiting for me on my person.

What I cannot recall is how I felt eating the cake. Maybe I was telling myself what a genius I was. I got them good.

\*\*\*

When my brother was old enough to drive, I begged him to take me to the old house. The first time I rang the bell, I explained that I was a former tenant. I couldn't believe how the house had changed. Even the front door was a different color. There was a distinct odor of cooking smells. I found that peculiar and wondered why I had never noticed smells like that in our house. Maybe we had a device that did away with kitchen odors?

The new owner was wearing shorts. I had no idea that grownups even wore shorts; I had never seen my mother wear shorts in my life. It felt too provocative and made me uncomfortable.

Literally nothing about the house, certainly not the décor, reminded me of yesteryear in that building.

The lady wasn't too keen on my snooping around amongst her things. After a few annoying intrusions like this, I got the message that I was no longer welcome to roam the scenes of my past. From then on, visits were restricted to my dream life.

Years ago, after we got up from my father's *shiva*, I decided I needed some serious closure with my past. After breaking his shoulder at seventy-five, my father had enlisted a driver, Nixon Chanoine, who became a beloved family friend. Nixon was still around, even though my father wasn't, and he was just what I needed, along with my dear friend Eva, who came in from Paris to walk me through my grief. The three of us made the journey to the house of my childhood.

I counted on Nixon to help us perform some amateur voodoo in order to loosen the hold the house still had on me. Nixon is Haitian, with an impressive knowledge of his culture's rituals. We must have looked pretty wacky standing in the snow, burning scraps of paper with writing in Patois that promised to sever the connection between me and all that the house called to mind.

Two years after my father's funeral, I was once again in America for a visit. I called Nixon, who was already well on his way to a new career in one of my father's projects. I told him I needed a voodoo booster, as I was still struggling with harsh memories. He came out one Sunday with his wife, Marie Flor. He winked when he told me she would put me right.

This might sound insane, but believe me—it happened. She stripped me naked and proceeded to paint me blue from head to toe. As she rinsed me off, she chanted words vaguely reminiscent of French. She then wrapped me in an old towel from my mother's linen closet. It was odd how dusty everything had become.

I wanted to believe in her magic. Unfortunately, it would take more years of psychological archeology for me to leave the past alone.

\* \* \*

I can remember the first of my last summers as a fat girl. I was fifteen. My parents and I were sitting on the back porch one Sunday, reading the camp section of the *New York Times*. My best friend, Stephanie, came over to visit. We had both been to marvelous camps the year before and were dying to have a summer together. Our parents vetoed the idea, so instead, we went on a shopping expedition through the *New York Times* to find the perfect camp for me.

Our parents had a hard time accepting our relationship. We were so close, so committed. Maybe our undying love inspired some jealousy in our mothers? Ev, my mother dearest, rolled her eyes whenever I mentioned Stephanie. She took every opportunity to badmouth Steph. We learned to accept our mothers' *mishegas*. We brushed it off, let it go and stopped trying to educate them. Stephanie and I knew we were forever.

I was still tall for my age and still overweight. I was not gross or obese, not by a long shot, but at that point in American history, my twenty-or-thirty-pound fatsuit made me feel bad about myself.

Stephanie found what she surmised to be the ideal solution to all my troubles: Camp Blah Blah for Overweight Girls. I actually bought the idea myself. It filled me with a heady sense of excitement. Just imagine this: I would go away for two months and come back skinny for the first time in my life. The plan was flawless.

I was so lucky to have Stephanie in my life. She was dedicated to my health and wellbeing in the cleanest and sincerest way. She knew that being chubby drove me nuts. I remember her saying so many times, "Elle, it's just my metabolism that makes me so skinny. Don't envy me, it's not healthy for our friendship."

On the night before I left, I called Stephanie and asked her to come over. There was an emergency abrew. I was starting to feel terribly, terribly frightened and overwhelmed. Before she could even ring the doorbell, I opened my window and burst out with this question: "Stepho, will I still be able to be funny if I lose weight?"

Well, look at that. I had already attached my identity to my bulk. I knew who I was with the extra weight; I was scared my personality might have to change to go along with my new look. And then who would I be?

She assured me that I could be whoever I wanted, regardless of the package. She gave me her blessing and off I went.

From the first day of camp, I knew I had made a mistake. To begin with, I was the thinnest camper in my bunk. I was surrounded by compulsive overeaters who were obviously worse off than I; being thinner, I triggered their resentment. This group was a conglomeration of teenage girls of never-seen-before sizes. I could hardly imagine where they came from, as I was one of the only heavy girls I knew.

The first night, my sleep was disturbed by the interminable rustling in the bed next to mine. I had been to camps before and had never had trouble sleeping. Exhausted after a lousy night, I questioned my neighbor on her nocturnal activity. She replied in the most matter-of-fact tone: "Oh, was I thrashing around? I'm sorry I disturbed you. I was hypnotized last week to break my habit of pulling my hair out of my head. I guess I cruise the area with my hand and then stop without pulling."

"Oh god," I thought, "she's not only morbidly obese, she's also insane. I hope she's not violent, too."

The truth is that as I was busy judging her and her multiple addictions, I was running a fast scan on myself for any similar weaknesses.

I was still a thumb-sucker. Even at the tender age of fifteen, I had enough psychological savvy to see the link between eating sweets and my compulsion to suck my thumb. In both cases, I was seeking solace by stuffing my mouth. My hand played a vital role in both of these events.

I decided right then and there that I would leave the thumb-sucking at camp. I never took the habit back, thank God.

About three weeks into the deal, I discovered that the little sap we had as a counselor—a skinny, scrawny country gal who had answered an ad—was hoarding candy bars in her cubbyhole. She obviously had the best metabolism on the planet and could stay thin in spite of all her sugary treats.

I was nobody's fool, right? How could I live knowing I was scarcely a yard away from my favorite chocolate insanity? I didn't even tell the other girls in the bunk because, from the look of it, they would have had a field day with my chocolate secret.

Eventually, I could not resist the temptation to steal a few. I felt guilty as hell for the thievery. In fact, I cannot remember ever stealing before or since. Breaking and entering into my own cupboards doesn't count.

That wasn't the worst of it. There was a drama counselor who took a shine to me and tried to seduce me one afternoon with the Barbara Streisand album *Funny Girl* and chocolate chip cookies. There were practically no two greater things in northern America for me at that time.

This lady played on my weaknesses and I found myself swimming in cookies. But my psychophysiology had undergone some fine-tuning in the last weeks; I had not only lost a lot of weight already, but had also rid my body of sugar and flour. Those cookies hit me like a bomb and I staggered out of her room with the excuse that I was nauseous.

I got back to my bunk in a sugared fog and lay down on the bed. I can't remember all the details, but in my stupor, I confessed the cookie orgy to my bunkmates. The counselor was fired that night because of this gross violation of camp ethics. I remember being very frightened that she would come back to the camp at night and murder me. I had never been involved in anything so big and complicated. Besides remorse for my eating, I felt guilty that she got fired–though I now recognize that she got her just desserts for singling me out and playing me like that. She knew what she was doing. She was older and had a plan.

My parents came for visiting day a week after the incident. I had managed to lose half of my extra weight by midsummer, and the change was breathtaking; I must have been quite a sight. The body of a fifteen-year-old, not terribly overweight to begin with, can undergo radical changes in a month of passionate dieting and exercise. I probably not only looked considerably thinner but had now become athletic, a completely new dimension to my physical self.

My parents didn't realize that I had had it with this camp. When I dropped the bomb that I was going home with them, they were adamant that I stay. They could see no logic to my insistence. In their eyes, this camp had delivered a miracle. Why would I deliberately flee before the transformation was brought to its completion?

The answer was that I was fed up. You may think that I had good reason to feel this way, but looking back, I see myself as more short-sighted and pigheaded than anything else. In spite of everything that went wrong, the camp delivered the goods. The results were stunning and probably would have become miraculous. With the offending counselor gone, I could have stayed on and finished the program.

Instead, I got stuck in a stubborn mindset that would not allow me to hear anything logical. I was really impossible, with very little self awareness. I made such a fuss, my parents had no recourse but to take me home.

As I ponder my behavior, I realize that I could conceivably have started my junior year of high school thin and beautiful. I opted to mastermind my own undoing. Bored to tears with nobody to hang out with over the second half of the summer, I gained most of the weight back.

Getting my own way was a Pyrrhic victory. All my friends were in camp; that was what all of us in the suburbs did in the summer. I had put myself in a stupid trap that left me with virtually nothing to do, no one to do it with, and a house full of food.

My parents worked all day and I was home with the maid. How many books could I devour in a day? I didn't have any hobbies, so I ate and watched TV. This had to be, barring none, the worst summer of my life. It was supposed to be my last summer as a fat girl.

As I think about it now, the *idea* of going to that camp was perfect. With the metabolism of a young adolescent, a diet of mostly vegetables, and a day brimming with physical activity, I was sure to become thin. Since that was the point, why did I need to sabotage all my fine efforts?

In truth, I wish someone on the staff had been wise enough to create a curriculum for us that addressed a fat girl's need to eat. Had that happened, I probably would not have fled so quickly. There were no support groups, individual counseling, or pep talks. In retrospect, I am surprised that my parents didn't inquire about this before sending me. Who knows? Maybe they thought if I could just take off the weight and be thin, I would stay thin.

There is some logic to this. I have heard of instances where young people have taken off extra weight without the benefit of psychological or spiritual intervention.

Basically, once they are on the right track, they enjoy their new bodies and self-images and savor them, never to become fat people again.

Who would I have become if I had taken off the weight when I was fifteen? I guess I'll never know the answer to that. So much of who I am, the crap and the greatness, is tied up with the life-long love affair I have with food.

\*\*\*

My next last summer as a fat girl was when I was hopelessly in love with Danny. I was going into my senior year of high school and he was a full six months younger. We were a ridiculous mismatch, but we had a soul connection that has bound us as friends to this day. The fact that I was close with a younger boy was scandalous, even though we weren't officially dating.

Though we both had brothers at Harvard, Danny's family was the absolute antithesis of mine. They were slim, highly restrained people who spoke in quiet tones and conducted themselves modestly. His mother was part of the Jewish aristocracy of pre-war Germany. I burst on the scene with my unbridled energy; it was too much for her.

Danny's father was a prolific artist whose canvases managed to convey the serenity that this man radiated. He painted in pastel hues I had never seen before in art. I was accustomed to darker, more somber colors.

But I was sixteen years old; what did I know about art? The few paintings and lithographs we had were old works, purchased on Sundays in Connecticut when my parents went antiquing. My mom would initiate these sprees, possibly as a way to divert my father from the golf course.

Danny was scheduled to be abroad for the whole summer. I made a decision that by the time he came back, I would be thin. This would truly be my last summer as a fat girl.

I begged my mother to help me. She was only too delighted, happy to ensure that I would be thin once and for all. Maybe she was envisioning some kind of scenario in which I would have a glorious senior year, get into an Ivy League college, and get out of her hair. Maybe then she could get on with her life. I know I was a thorn in her side; I know that her menopause and my adolescence were mortal enemies. We were the most combustible chemistry imaginable.

That June, she hand-delivered me to Dr. Greenberg on 57th Street.

After waiting for hours in his office, I was finally admitted to the inner sanctum. I was thirty-two pounds overweight with a big, fresh mouth. I was sassy with the doctor and told him: "For a wait like that, I was expecting the Wizard of Oz."

You know what? He was the Wizard of Oz. Dr. Greenberg literally took away my appetite. I got what I came for—a complete transformation in only two months.

This was the age of innocence. I knew nothing about drugs or prescription medicine. I did what I was told and the Wizard of Oz worked his magic.

My senior year of high school was amazing. I felt good. I looked good. It was all coming together for me and I was riding high. I was also high on amphetamines, but I didn't know that.

I still loved eating but found that a few bites did the trick. I had no sense of being on a diet. I know I wasn't watching my food. I felt above hunger for the first time in my life.

As I look back on my behavior then, I see that I was clearly manic. I was larger than life, audacious. I took senseless risks. I was a handful, but tremendously loving, funny and bright.

I never questioned how Dr. Greenberg's pills worked. I assumed he knew that. He was a doctor; I trusted him, as I did all the doctors I had ever been to. They went to medical school, they knew about my body. The success was written all over me. I was in heaven.

About fifteen months after I began seeing Dr. Greenberg, I was on my way to the airport to fly off to college. My parents gave my friends permission to drive me, using my car. It was a second-hand Impala convertible that I got in my senior year of high school. We put the top down and cruised out of town with loud Latin music blasting.

These guys, affectionately called Elmo and Gizmo, were two of the most outrageous characters I have ever met, totally irreverent and bold. I remember one time they peeled the label off a box of suppositories that my mother had in the refrigerator and affixed it to a banana: "Insert rectally as needed." Those guys were nuts. I loved them madly.

On the way out of my neighborhood, they screamed: "Eat your hearts out, Scarsdale! The Earth Mother is leaving!"

The boys had named me "the Earth Mother" when I was sixteen. After a few months, the name stuck and everyone called me that, even my friends' parents. Some of them don't remember my real name to this day.

Elmo and Gizmo were forever foraging in my

pocketbook; I let them. Before we got to the airport, they found my medication. I must have been given several months' supply. Their eyes lit up and they begged me to give them half my pills. They were skinny and I couldn't understand what all the excitement was about.

I was already thin and I figured I didn't need the pills anymore. I remember giving them everything without a second thought.

\* \* \*

My great undoing at the University of Wisconsin was that I didn't have the slightest idea how to take care of myself. Besides for summer camp and a little jaunt to Israel, I was a seventeen-year-old kid who was used to her parents tucking her in. By the way, I mean this literally. I used to yell from my bed, "Who will administer the pat-outs?"

Often my father would recite a prayer with me and sing me a lullaby. His mother did this with him; I did it with my children.

I was not prepared for life on a sprawling college campus. The fact that I had no accountability blew me away. I could go to class; I could skip class. Hundreds of students peopled the lecture halls–I was never missed.

I had never cut classes in high school. I don't know whether it was my sense of ethics, my respect for the teachers, or the fear that my parents would get a note. I simply never, ever did it.

But now I was virtually on my own and I was given the following instructions by all the lecturers: "Here is the reading list, the exam is in January. Good luck." Good

God! How was I supposed to know how to handle this? I was grossly ill-prepared for learning in this manner.

I took a natural science class. I sat in a steeply-sloped lecture hall and the teacher spoke from the pit below. Week after week, it became increasingly clear that I did not know my ass from my elbow. I just doodled on my jeans, whose waistband soon began to dig into me. Other courses, which should have been in my mother tongue, English, used nomenclature with which I was unfamiliar. I found myself struggling to keep up.

High school had been a completely different matter. The classes were small and intimate. The assignments were clear. When I was given homework, I did it promptly and joyfully. I felt a great sense of mastery. Here at the university, there were no workbooks to fill in and no mimeographed sheets to do. I was without guidelines. I was without guidance. I was without my pills and I was getting hungry.

So I did what I always did, only much worse.

My mother wasn't there to scowl at me and make me feel like a swine for taking an extra portion. My mother wasn't around, period. I had no one to fight with and no one to set me straight, either. I guess that's when the inner monsters began to reappear.

Within months, none of my clothes fit. I couldn't believe it. The notion that I was finally thin forever, finished with the shame of overeating and overweight, went up in smoke.

Apropos of smoke, everyone at college was heavily involved with marijuana and hallucinogenics. I was never a pothead, but if I was at a party and someone offered a joint, I took it. The munchies had their way with me and within six months of starting college, I had put back on all the weight and then some.

By the spring, I had amassed a huge circle of friends and thirty-five pounds of unwanted blubber. I had also developed severe lower back pains and wound up in the university hospital. They gave me daily injections of Valium, a drug I had never heard of. I held court in the hospital, hosting visitors and well-wishers.

Ten days into my hospital stay, there were student riots and political protests. Not one to miss a good event, I left the hospital against medical orders. The morning's Valium injection was doing its job; I felt supremely confident and relaxed about my decision.

Two days later, in agonizing pain, I hobbled into the emergency room. Somehow, I snuck a peek at my file. I still remember the humiliation I felt when I read the words "psychosomatic pain suspected." I was eighteen years old, on my own in the Midwest, totally unprepared for the exams coming up and totally devastated by the idea that the pain was actually in my head. I went back to the dorm, called my parents and said I was coming home.

I packed my bags. And because I knew my parents were leaving in two days for a vacation, I packed a separate suitcase for the trip. I naturally assumed they were taking me with them. As I write this I am still amazed at my unmitigated gall.

When my dad picked me up from JFK and I told him how excited I was for the trip, he threw me a look that said: "Are you kidding?"

Rarely angry with me, my dad did not hold back this time. He told me in no uncertain terms that I was not getting any prizes for this little fiasco. I had dropped out of college, nothing to be proud of. I was not even allowed to stay at our house with the maid. No, I had to stay at Ida's—my sister-in-law's mother. According to my parents, I had to find a job, enroll in summer school and get my act together.

I did what I was told and straightened myself out. I lived on cigarettes and low calorie sodas. By summer's end, I was more or less OK. I had dieted almost all the excess weight off. I had even managed to finagle my way into NYU.

\* \* \*

It was at NYU summer school that I had my first encounter with a real, live anorexic. She looked absolutely skeletal. She insisted on wearing little sundresses, though her shoulder blades were so prominent that they looked like wings. Her knees were just covered bones. Her cheek and jaw didn't look like anything I had seen before on a live human being—well, maybe in photographs of Holocaust victims or Biafrans. I am ashamed to say now that before Susan and I became friends, I was part of a little group of elitist snobs who called her "the skinny girl." If this group of snot-nosed prigs had seen me two months before, they would have called me "the pig."

That year, as a sophomore living in the NYU dorms, I developed a particular hankering for meat sandwiches and Napoleons. I was lucky that things stayed reasonably under control. Somehow, I managed to hold my weight steady for that first year. I can't remember how I pulled it off; I never did any formal exercise. But I was without a car and that forced me and my *toochas* to walk.

My parents invited me to join them on the trip they took the next summer. One afternoon, bored and lonely in the guesthouse where we were staying, I felt an irresistible craving for food.

It didn't occur to me to find something to do in town or take myself to a movie. No, I wanted to eat.

I was embarrassed to order a whole meal from the luncheonette on the corner. I settled on a basket of dinner rolls and butter.

So–very nonchalantly–I ordered my little snack, five rolls in all. I gobbled them down with such haste that I practically choked. I was afraid I'd get busted. I remember this scene vividly. It was neither my first nor my last on-the-sly gobble.

That much white flour knocked me out and back in my room, I fell into a deep sleep. When I awoke, I rushed to assemble myself for dinner. Our dinners were always formal affairs. They required the proper attire, meaning a dress, stockings and–at my mother's insistence–an old-fashioned, unforgiving girdle.

That evening, I remember trying to stuff myself into the girdle. I had a crazy idea that those five rolls had fattened me up a few sizes. I was sweating bullets. Feeling guilty and ashamed, I confessed my sins at dinner. My mother was furious; her face took on that all-too-familiar look of disgust. It was something she mastered in the muscles around her mouth and her eyes. She could have been a mime. She pursed her lips as if she was about to whistle; she twisted them off to the side and it looked like she had something on her lip she wanted to chew off. Her eyes turned to slits.

It was all done so quickly, like the sleight of hand of a magician. It was meant only for me, so she had to be stealthy.

What a painful moment. My dad, as always, stuck up for me, fielding all my mother's insults and blows. He kept trying to explain that I had committed no great crime. She was pushing him to see how self-destructive I was. She was relentless. I couldn't look at either of them. I had failed us all so miserably.

By the next year, I could not even get one leg into the pants I bought on that trip.

\* \* \*

In the fall of my junior year, I was all of nineteen years old and was set to room with an old acquaintance from high school. Living in that apartment with Francine and her dog Clarence was outrageous. We kept nonsensical hours and did what we pleased, with no one around to stop us. We went bowling after midnight, saw artsy fartsy movies in Greenwich Village and attended protest marches whenever they were held.

Actually, some of my behavior was being monitored by my psychoanalyst, Sidney. He was the treasure I received from my mother for my twentieth birthday, the first half of a two-part present. I spent much of my junior and senior years on his couch in Riverdale.

Part two was a referral for a new diet doctor who came recommended by my brother and sister-in-law. With my mother's blessing, I made weekly trips to Port Chester in my brand new car, Velveeta Volvo. I had séances there with a very peculiar man who gave me injections. My desire for food was completely lifted and after six months, I stopped *schlepping* up to see him. It was, again, another version of me lacking follow-through.

For some reason, I never thought to tell Sidney about the diet doctor.

It would surely have been appropriate. My analysis with Sidney consisted of my psycho-history as an overeater, my sense memories of food and my problematic body image. I had been ashamed of my legs all my life; I remember lying on Sidney's leather couch, raising my legs in the air and posing the question: "Sidney, will these legs ever straighten out?" I asked this because I truly did not know the answer. I don't remember what he said, but I remember being deeply concerned that I was somehow disfigured.

I conducted some of my psychoanalysis in song, prancing around what had to be one of the most dramatic psychiatric offices in the world. Sidney had a two-story, cathedral-ceilinged clinic with a stained-glass wall. It's possible that I was in that clinic no less than a hundred times over those two years, since psychoanalysis requires a minimum of five sessions a week. True to the rules set forth by Freud, most of the work took place with me lying down on my back, Sidney out of my visual field. Sometimes, though–between brilliant insights, detailed recollections of dreams and past humiliations–I snooped around the office. The stained glass wall was so unlike the biblical-themed kind I'd seen in synagogues and churches. It was merely decorative and colorful and so much more than a window. It was a bold, eyebrow-raising way to deal with a wall.

It was a look that I so adored, I later had my

husband–artist and architect of our home–build us a living space too similar to be coincidental.

Sidney sat behind me, never taking notes, patiently smoking a pipe or a cigarette. He always wore loafers and crossed his legs. His shoes were casual, yet very pricey. No matter what shirt and tie he donned, he always wore gray pants and navy blue socks. My dad, the only other grownup man I knew, wore suits and highly polished tie shoes exclusively. Sidney never wore a suit. My father never wore loafers.

I felt that Sidney was my friend and that I could take enormous liberties. I had unbelievable *chutzpah*. I cannot count the number of times I reached back behind me and pulled on his navy blue socks. His legs were surprisingly hairless for a man with a pompadour.

* * *

The summer before my senior year at NYU was a disaster. I contracted mononucleosis from kissing a beau in Central Park, an on-again, off-again flame with whom I liked sparring about politics. He was an interesting fellow, but severely dysfunctional. He had a nasty streak and I suspected he took a perverse delight in handing me his mono.

I've been told that most people lose weight with the kind of sore throat this disease brings. Not in my case. A self-soother from way back, I wasn't going to let the pain in my throat stop me. I found cooling foods to slide down my raw, achy, tonsil-less throat. It took me one month to gain twenty-five pounds.

I moved home to be nursed back to health. My parents

were never in the house before six o'clock in the evening and I was left in the care of the housekeeper, who didn't know me all that well. I mostly did my own thing, namely, watching TV and eating.

Sometime in August, when I no longer had mono, my parents looked at me across the dinner table and realized that I had swelled up again. They remembered that Judge Wikler, our old neighbor, had gone somewhere in the Midwest to lose weight. When my parents asked, he told them about a sanitarium in Michigan. I was on a plane two days later.

Battle Creek was a joke. I declined to eat in the dining room and by the third day had manipulated the staff into letting me eat in my room instead. This was outrageous and unheard of, but I pulled it off. I am shocked and horrified as I recall that I got this institution, this paragon of nutritious eating, to bow to my demands for an all-protein diet. They served me well-done hamburgers and cottage cheese on demand.

I also had daily sessions under steaming hot blankets. I came to adore this part of the weight-loss program,.

Almost all the people at this clinic were antiques. There's no other way to describe them. I was twenty and they were old, ailing codgers.

As is my way, I made an executive decision to flee after two weeks and ordered the most expensive cab ride of my life thus far.

Although I did shed some pounds in Michigan, it was an unimpressive feat. I would gain them all back before school started in the fall.

\*\*\*

My senior year at NYU was a real mish-mash. My saving grace was the fact that there were political protests on campuses all across America and classes switched to a pass/fail system. All I needed to do was pass; somehow, I wound up on the Dean's List.

One of the best parts of my senior year was a summer session in Israel. I stopped in Paris on the way. I was a little too heavy to shop there for clothes, so I settled on a *chapeau*. I always had a great face for hats.

I wasn't on diet medicine at that point, but I was taking a thyroid booster that my mom put me on at an early age. She had the idea it would help me metabolize more quickly and somehow got the doctor to comply. I took it for thirteen years. I vividly recall pouring all my thyroid medication on the floor of a swanky Parisian hotel in order to make sure I had enough pills to get through the summer.

Two years after Paris, when I actually had my thyroid tested, it was clear I was not hypo-thyroid. All this monkeying around with my hormones might explain why I had such a rough ride during menopause.

That summer, while I did little to advance my knowledge of the Hebrew language, I was a giant social success. I had an intense and exciting two months.

Room and board included three meals a day. Despite the heat, the meals were heavy and rich. Massive amounts of grease were laced through everything. I tried to develop a technique to keep myself distanced from the daily onslaught; I put black pepper on the food, hoping it would turn me off. But I was too crafty and circumvented the peppery top of every mashed potato mountain, managing to eat all that lay underneath.

My cravings were simply non-negotiable. If it were not for the fact that, having no car, I had to walk a lot, I would have really blown up that summer.

\* \* \*

I came back to Israel again the next summer. I had spent the previous year in a one-room studio in Greenwich Village, taking some graduate courses in psychology at NYU. This did not help me much with finding a direction in life. I had no clear path for my professional future. In an effort to delay any serious commitments, I agreed to join a one-year domestic peace corps program and got myself a posting in the north of Israel, at the Lebanese and Syrian borders.

I stopped going to Hebrew classes after the first week. Except for eating, I cannot tell you what I did all day. I discovered a bunch of restaurants in the town's center. Recklessly, with absolutely no regard for consequence, I ate.

Food ruled. Although it didn't taste like what I knew and loved in America, I made do. There were numerous occasions that summer when strangers came up to me in the street, watched me devour a snack or a meal in a pita, and said the Hebrew version of *bon appétit,* which literally means "hearty appetite." Such a thing was completely alien to my American upbringing and the words always sounded slightly cynical and nasty to me. No one on the streets of America would salute a stranger in the middle of a hotdog.

It would be especially unheard of to offer such a comment to an overweight individual.

I am not saying that I wouldn't notice an overweight young woman, bursting at the seams, stuffing her cheeks with food that she needed like a hole in her head. Believe me, I make very detailed remarks in my internal monologue. Here I have to fault my father. Although a very spiritually gifted individual, he delivered a running commentary on everything in his visual field: "Can you imagine how such a slob can tie his shoes? And he *has* to eat those two hotdogs?" "Did you see that woman driving that car full of children? Do you believe she has the *chutzpah* to smoke with all of them there?" He whispered these comments to me, taking care that the person he was talking about never heard it. They were meant to be astute observations, not insults.

It was contagious—all this criticism. In a crowd, I am capable of assessing everyone, on every level, from moral to aesthetic.

What I didn't understand was that in the Middle East, Israel specifically, people have something to say about everything. They do not hesitate to say it to your face.

\*\*\*

Things only got much worse through the fall and winter and by January, I hit my all-time high: two hundred and two pounds. Today, two-hundred pound adults are hardly a rarity, but back then, those extra fifty pounds overwhelmed me.

Nothing turned out according to plan. I had gone off

to Israel thinking I was destined to be the next Golda Meir. I was confident that I would master the Hebrew language and find my true nature and purpose. There was no doubt in my mind that I would take Israel by storm. I had a B.A. in the pocket of my jeans and the energy of a pioneer.

But food had other ideas, clouding my thinking and distorting my self-image. I turned into a version of myself I didn't much fancy. I saw that I was just this side of depressed and was going to have to buy time until I could shake off the blues and find my center.

While all my friends from the *ulpan* (Hebrew language school) wound up in development towns, I finagled a placement in a picturesque village in the Galilee called Rosh Pina. It was teaming with hippies and expatriates. The scene was quite international. It was a virtual Tower of Babel.

I started out offering my services as an English teacher and/or social worker, though I didn't have any formal training in either of these realms. Within a few weeks of my placement at the local school, I slithered away. I can't imagine how I got out of working. I must have made up some semi-reasonable excuse.

Nobody else seemed to have a job. The bohemian community of Rosh Pina was at that time heavily into marijuana and acid. By the grace of God, I was spared from getting too involved. I dabbled very rarely, cautious not to throw my delicate brain into any God-forsaken territories. Mind-altering substances seemed way too risky. Food was my thing. I did not want to pick up another escape.

That fall and winter weren't easy times for me. Everyone I knew was stoned from morning to night. This made self-proclaimed philosophers out of otherwise fairly ordinary people. While they all thought they were enlightened, they were more misguided than my friends back home.

Eventually, I got fed up with the scene and with the blob I had become. I retreated to my home and ate. I had no scale and somehow most of my clothes stretched with me, sort of. I was spilling out in every direction—my appearance a metaphor for how I was feeling inside.

After so many years of relative independence, it was humiliating to have no other option but my parents' house. But I had nowhere else to go.

\* \* \*

My homecoming was hardly a joyful matter for any of us. My poor parents absolutely didn't know what to do with me. This was not like the defeat of my freshman year, when I dropped out of college. Then, I was eighteen and malleable. They told me to get a job, get into summer school and shape up. I was compliant, following directions and straightening myself out.

No, this was an entirely different matter. I was twenty-three, a college graduate with a B.A. in American Literature and a few graduate courses in psychology. There was nothing I could do with that. I was hardly trained in anything. Besides, my spirits were so low, I had no wherewithal or motivation to do anything.

As my mother saw it, the first challenge was to get the weight off as quickly as possible. Maybe then I would regain my spirit and turn this disaster around. I wasn't about to go back to Battle Creek, but she'd heard about a different radical weight loss place in upstate New York.

For two weeks, all I ingested was water. The place was creepy. I don't know how I survived. When my stay was up, I had lost twenty-five pounds. Even the staff was astounded.

I got in my car and went to visit a friend in New Haven who was studying at Yale. He was in medical school and living on breakfast cereal and sandwiches. The switch to carbohydrates must have shocked my entire psychophysiology. I was still disoriented when I got back to my parents' house two days later. I think my parents thought I was drugged.

In no time, I was almost back up to the grotesquerie of two hundred and two pounds. This time the consensus was to send me to an endocrinologist.

I remember sitting for hours in a medical testing facility. I had to ingest a very sweet liquid at periodic intervals. The tests came back showing that there was nothing significantly wrong with my metabolism.

The problem was my spirits. I was on my way into a profound melancholia that was exacerbated by being fat. Eating provided a temporary feeling of elation and wellbeing that was inevitably chased by lethargy.

\* \* \*

So there I was, twenty-three years old, back in my parents' house after six years on my own (not including the one-month recovery from mono). What a mess.

In those days, my mother and I graduated to a love-hate relationship. We were best with a good geographical spread between us. Seeing me up close must have been trying. I had turned into a fat slob; she was particularly repulsed by fat slobs.

How can I fault her for this? Years later, my mom told me that as *her* mother lay dying in her arms, she whispered: "Evelyn, my life, my love, don't let your kid sister Cynthia get fat."

I know today, as a wife and mother, that seeing your loved ones struggling is hard to bear. You secretly wish they would wake up and get over themselves. That must have been part of my mother's *schtick*. It had to have been hell for her to hear me cry about being fat and promise I was going to straighten myself out–and then witness me taking a nosedive back into the fridge.

\*\*\*

In the spring of that year, an old friend began a relentless campaign to get me to learn how to meditate. I don't remember why he was around. No one else was. It was pretty slim pickings for me back then. All my friends were well-settled in graduate schools, generally not in the New York area.

Andy Lynton made me his project. Neither of us had a clue as to how blue I truly was. I was still chatty and amusing. It's hard to imagine how I managed to disguise my enormous *weltschmerz*, a term for world-weariness. Just to look at me, young and swollen, should have been a tip-off.

The song that kept me alive through that period of my life was "It's Going to Take Some Time" by Carole King. This song reinforced the idea that there is a necessary process to change and that time is an enormous factor. Just recently I found the journal I kept then. I repeatedly refer to Carole King as my cheerleader.

Andy Lynton, God bless his soul, was a dog with a bone. My mother even agreed to come with me to take the Transcendental Meditation (TM) course, though she told me to check it out before she would commit. I don't think she especially believed she would become a meditator.

Want to know something crazy and wonderful? Six weeks before her death, my little sweetheart of a mother told me and my son Shimon, who was freshly back from an *ashram* in India, what her mantra was. It took her twenty-eight years to tell. What a rascal. I still can't bring myself to do the same. I've said the same mantra for years and no one knows it but me.

Andy came to the front door to take me to the preliminary lecture. This was one of those ridiculous *nothing* days where I promised my parents at breakfast I would try to get myself together. Naturally, the minute they left for work, life and meaning in New York City, I settled myself down in front of the television and prepared for the usual systematic self-destruction. That which we know as activity, challenge or hobby was basically not part of my repertoire during this, the bleakest period of my life. I was not interested in socializing; I could not bear how I looked. I holed myself up in my parents' house in the suburbs and watched the hours drag by.

Television and food. Food and television. As long as I had enough of both, I could live through the day. Each, in its own way, kept me reasonably numb.

On this spring day, I had manipulated the maid into

preparing a gourmet rendition of that old classic, macaroni and cheese. I gobbled down enough to reach my own personal level of satiation. I comfortably forgot that that *nudnik* Andy Lynton was due to come over in the late afternoon. I daresay that I was still in my flannel nightgown when he showed up. I think I burped upon opening the door to Andy.

He was very cool when I told him that there was no way I was *schlepping* to an introductory TM lecture. He didn't bat an eyelash when he informed me that there was another lecture scheduled in two days and that we could go then.

I will remember that moment for the rest of my life. I realized I was screwed; by hook or by crook, meditation was clearly my fate. Salvation had rung my front doorbell and was willing to take whatever time was required.

I went two days later with Andy, this time with my mother in tow. It astounds me that he had the patience to sit through this intro for the umpteenth time. He didn't seem to care. He was on a mission to save my soul. Andy was so into the Maharishi and his enthusiasm was infectious.

What the Maharishi said on those films made sense to my mother and me. When were we ever in the presence of a white-robed man teaching about bliss consciousness and freedom from emotional traps? He touched us as a scholar, scientist and enlightened human being. It was obvious, right there and then, that we were in for the whole deal. Have I mentioned that my mother was an incredibly astute and intellectually-gifted woman, not easily impressed?

After that first meeting, my mom and I dutifully continued to attend and waited patiently for the day when we would actually learn how to practice TM rather than learn about its benefits.

On July 8th, Mom and I received our mantras. This practice turned my entire life around, hoisting me up from the longest and foulest depression I have ever known. I can't remember a day since on which I have skipped a morning meditation.

Miracle of miracles, six weeks after I started meditating, I read an article in the *New York Times* about recent advances in the field of psycho-linguistics. The research sounded so interesting that I made a mad dash to study the subject in some formal manner in New York. Less than two months into daily meditation and I knew I had my mind back. I knew I could trust myself. I knew I would be fine. I found a way to sneak into a program at NYU in order to pursue this wacky dream of learning about the development of language.

That September, I made a contract with my parents. I still have it today in my top drawer. The deal: I had to lose fifty pounds and finish the year with a master's degree–no small accomplishment. Don't forget, I had already taken some graduate courses in psychology. For their part, they would pay for school and fully support me for the duration.

Another feature of their part of the bargain was that my mother had to start believing I was capable of change. I could hardly blame her for her lack of faith; I had a lot to prove to myself, too. I knew as well as she did that I hardly finished anything I started. I knew as well as she did that historically, I couldn't be counted on.

In the fall of that year, I embarked on a journey that promised to take me closer to my true nature and purpose.

It took some time for my beloved mother to believe her eyes, but a year later I was no longer the mess who signed the contract. I was slimmer than she ever dreamed and on top of that, I had a master's degree and a job at one of the most respected scientific institutions in the world–Rockefeller University.

A year before, I knew nothing about developmental psychology. Now I was being paid to investigate child language acquisition. Yes, I was a rookie, I was the youngest and most inexperienced kid on the block, but I lived in the neighborhood. My mother had no choice but to start believing. Maybe, just maybe, I was turning into something worth her love and respect.

I have to say that, except for a few unpleasant skirmishes, she and I stayed gorgeous together from this point until she passed away.

\*\*\*

Three summers after we signed the contract was my last summer as a single girl. What a time I had. I left New York and shuttled back and forth between my beau Howie in Berkeley and Stephanie in L.A. I had finished all my doctoral coursework and was in the middle of my thesis. I had job interviews in San Francisco and San Diego. My weight had been low for two years and I was on top of the world.

I was heavier than Stephanie all of our lives together and that summer was no exception. While she marched around in her tiny little shorts, I was sort of radiant in my pantsuits. Look, what can I say? I've never looked stunning in a mini skirt. I've always carried my weight in my legs.

## The Early Years

\*\*\*

In the fall, I took a position working with senior citizens. I wanted a break from the theoretical; I was given the opportunity to work with people, get into their souls a little and get paid for it to boot. My dad had recently built a large health-related facility near my apartment in Brooklyn Heights and offered me a job. Even though I was the boss's daughter and could have cut corners whenever I wanted, I took my job seriously and deeply respected the privilege of working with the patients.

I was twenty-five years old when I realized that my true destiny lay in helping people learn how to be happy. My formal training would come almost a decade later, when I studied family and couples therapy at Tel Aviv University. By that time, I already had three children at home and one on the way.

If I were looking from above, I might notice a very distinct pattern ruling my life that wasn't always clear while I was living it. For example, in the spring prior, I had visited a Russian fortune-teller's studio. I was walking on a street in Greenwich Village on my way back from class when a young woman beckoned to me from the second floor. She looked innocent enough and I was characteristically a risk-taker. When I entered her place, she asked if I wanted my palm or tarot cards read. I told her both. For twenty-five dollars and my first experience with a professional soothsayer, I was ready to go for broke. She proceeded to tell me that I was about to face a big disappointment. It would involve a journey and a great shock. I was already greatly shocked by the fact that she knew I about to take a trip to the West Coast;

I had plane tickets for L.A. and San Francisco in my bag. There was no way she could have known that. This was my first big encounter with that certain kind of *knowing* that is impossible to fathom. She told me that the fellow I was going to visit had fallen in love with a dark-haired, dark-skinned woman with five children.

She told me that I had nothing to worry about because I had already met the man I was to marry, a foreigner who would take me to his country. She saw me having excellent relations with his mother. She also said that we would have four children and lead a happy and extraordinary life.

I left her rooms, went down to the street and looked for a payphone. I called my father because he was the right person to hear this. I told Stephanie about this freaky encounter too, when I got to L.A. two days later. She didn't make much of it until I called Howie in Berkeley to finalize the arrangements for the weekend. He told me he'd come to L.A. instead. My jaw must have hit my knees. Stephanie stared in disbelief as Howie explained about his new relationship with a widowed (and actually divorced before her ex-husband died) African American mother of five.

What are the odds? What, in God's name, are the odds that this unknown Russian woman would have the power to tap into my life in such unparalleled ways? I called my father again, this time waking him up because of the three-hour time difference between L.A. and New York, and said: "Daddy, forgive me, but you will never believe this. Howie really has fallen for a lady with five kids." My father, without skipping a beat, with no sleep in his tone, reminded me about the second part of the vision. My husband-to-be was on the horizon, already in my life.

## The Early Years

\*\*\*

After the best summer ever on the West Coast, I was writing my doctoral thesis and working in the health facility that my father owned. I had the distinct privilege of seeing a lot of my father at the office. It had been years since I saw him on a daily basis. I treasured those moments.

In October, I went to visit my darling friend Danny for the weekend. He was at Harvard Medical School and we were as close as ever. Remember, he was my great love in high school.

On the flight back from Boston I had the uncanny urge to rearrange my space and clear it of childish memorabilia. My shelves were cluttered with presents I had gotten over the years. My apartment was too cute and inappropriate for my age. I gathered all the silliness and made a bag for a friend of mine who was a single parent. Oddly relieved and noticeably more adult, I strutted around the apartment feeling ready to face a mature set of challenges.

I called a friend who lived a few neighborhoods away, in a commune of Israeli students, and asked if I could come over and meditate with him. Meditating in the presence of another human being adds to the power of the experience.

He fell asleep during the meditation, so I let myself out of the room quietly, without disturbing him. As I was edging the door back into a closed position, carefully easing the handle into place, Michael appeared. I was so excited that I fell down. Michael was a very busy person and I almost never saw him on my visits to the commune.

As Michael hoisted me up from my tumble, he asked me if I was hungry. Can you imagine asking *me* such a question? I replied: "Always," kind of pushing that one word out of the back of my throat, seductive and cute all at once.

As it happened, he had given a dinner party the night before. The leftovers were plentiful, tasty and aesthetic, served on plates he had made. I couldn't recall ever having been dined like that before. So many years later, I even remember the ceramics. They were rough blue plates with inlaid cutlery; he had pushed a fork, knife and spoon into the wet clay to leave an impression.

After dinner, he took me on a grand tour of the house. His artwork was everywhere. I had never personally seen such a range. Not that I was so experienced in the world of art, but I could not fail to notice all the dazzling sculptures, pottery pieces and remarkably daring jewelry. It just didn't stop. He was a master in metal, clay, fiberglass and rubber. Here and there, I even saw whimsical pieces of glass he had done. This guy was a true Renaissance genius.

The first time I had laid eyes on him was at my friend Renata's. We didn't exchange a word; I was too busy catching up with some of the other guests, whom I already knew. It was the fall after I learned to meditate, the autumn of that contract with my parents. He was a young Israeli studying sculpture and architecture in New York.

A year and a half later, I saw him again at Renata's. This time it was her birthday. I distinctly recall giving her a pair of orange, high-topped sneakers; he laughed when she took them out of the box. We caught each other's gaze and he indicated that he remembered me by gesturing with his hands that I had lost a significant amount of weight. I was a good fifty pounds thinner and much more attractive.

We did not speak; he was somewhat shy, with his poor English. Although I had been to Israel several times, my Hebrew was rusty at best.

The next time we met was at the commune. I was there with Stephanie and Renata and he was busy hosting. This time, he was linguistically adept and more confident. I noticed that he was also very handsome. Yikes, was he handsome!

Now here was I, standing beside him, viewing endless works of art after having eaten such tasty food off those handmade plates. I didn't personally know any other young men who could host me on this level. It was hard to concentrate on the tour.

Not to be outdone, I told him I had something great to show him. I had to come up with something no less impressive. So, what did I do? I *schlepped* him to the care center where I worked. I had never been there after hours. It was an entirely different scene. A number of my patients, all of whom were in wheelchairs, were waiting at the elevators to be taken up to bed. This bunch of weary-looking figures came alive when they saw me enter: "Ellie! Ellie is here!" They sprang up in those chairs, shouting for joy. I thought I would die of pride. I had known I was important to them, but this welcome was huge.

Michael still recalls the scene. He says he knew then that he loved me.

After a few days that included two art openings, a Pirandello play, a few shared meals and the privilege of hearing him read the *Torah* on the Sabbath, we drove up to Scarsdale, New York to have lunch with my parents.

When we finished the meal, my dad whisked him

away to the den and read him some passages in Yiddish. What possessed my father to do this remains a mystery. Nevertheless, after half an hour together, they came out smiling. A bond had been created. My father knew that my soul mate had arrived; in a phone call the next morning, he advised me to marry Michael.

There aren't so many details to our courtship, as we tied the knot in three weeks.

I'm not saying there are no charlatans out there, but that Russian clairvoyant clearly knew my destiny.

# Dear Diary: The Experiment June-September

## *June 26ᵗʰ*

That's it. I've had it.

This is not healthy and I can't put off facing it any longer. I must do something to stop the insanity. I've gotten too far in life to wind up weighted down by my own hand. It's inappropriate for someone such as I, who has done so much work on herself.

How did I ever let this happen? It's not as if I woke up one morning and discovered I was fat. Such a thought is ridiculous.

I've got to take this seriously. I'm going to have to put a lot of effort into this adventure. I need to be brave and conscientious and scrupulously scientific about what I am doing in order to liberate myself from the piled-up pounds.

I desperately wanted to be precise and coincide with the onset of the season (summer officially began on the 21st of June). It's the 26th and I am five days behind schedule. If this truly is to be my last summer as a fat girl, I have to get the ball rolling.

I vow to work my twelve-step program of Overeaters Anonymous honestly and rigorously. I have been a member for over two decades now, with the same sponsor for almost all that time. Like they say in the program, it works when you work it–so work it–you're worth it. I am worth taking proper heed of the psycho-spiritual aspect of my relationship with food.

I also hereby commit to a physical exercise regimen. Today I begin a daily tryst with the exercise bicycle. I know that it will be difficult and conceivably unpleasant in the beginning. I know I have to hand this huge task over to the universe, which always supports my greater good. I am a novice, pledging to pedal twenty minutes at a reasonable speed. Even if my heart is pounding and I am sweating like a racehorse, I know I will get better over time.

I pledge to join Weight Watchers, attending weekly meetings and weigh-ins.

I will monitor this experiment by keeping a diary, citing my successes and failures. Having learned how to free associate on Sidney's couch, I will gleefully resume the position and recline while dictating my entries to my assistant, Shani. Her hands will type my words. Just like Sidney, she will be witness to my free associations, never interrupting or commenting until I have finished each section.

Thirty years ago, I discovered that I can speak while

I meditate. I will take advantage of this skill in order to dictate exclusively from this special state of consciousness.

So here I am at the beginning, eating a bag of farewell M&Ms as I talk. I am wondering why they do not remotely match my expectations. They bear almost no resemblance to the recipe that was produced in my childhood, the M&Ms of yesteryear. They even taste extremely fake and chemically altered, but of course I am nearing the end of the bag.

I guess I have a pretty big nerve thinking I can write a book about recovery.

Of late, my weight is hovering at a personal high. It is the second time in my life that I am this heavy. Nothing has helped me overcome the relentless urge to gobble. No insight, no wisdom, no loving look, no compassion, no disgust—none of them have succeeded in getting me to lay down my arms in this battle.

"Lay down my arms." What would it be like to literally lay down my arms and stop stuffing food in my mouth?

## *July 2nd*

In the space of a few days, the universe has decided to show me two diametrically opposed examples of eating disorders. The timing is perfect. I could not imagine a louder cheering squad from above than a higher power that would confront me with these two blatant examples of how something as innocent as food could turn into something so perverse.

The first is a new patient who has joined the rehab group I lead. I am used to all manner of appearances in my clients, but this is truly breathtaking. This thirtyish, articulate young woman takes the cake as the thinnest upright being on two legs I have ever seen. The universe undoubtedly sent her to me bearing the message that even thin women can go too far, as if I didn't know that already. But I cannot afford the luxury of forgetting how bad it can be. I should carry a picture of her around with me as a reminder.

I pray that I will be able to help her, that through the mire of my own food struggles, I can give some glimmer of hope, some taste of recovery.

I am not entirely sure that she belongs at our rehab. We are not set up to cater to such blatant medical matters. But I guess she's made the rounds of so many other institutions that did not help her; maybe she's hoping our approach will do the trick. If she tastes recovery, if she embraces the Twelve Steps, she has a chance of becoming well and looking like it.

If her example isn't powerful enough, I can always feast on Thursday night reruns of *The Biggest Loser*. Funny title for a show. It's meant to be cute; it's a play on words to describe a weight-loss contest, giving the prize to the individual who succeeds in losing the most weight. Usually, he or she is the biggest, fattest one in the competition.

Last night, ten very obese American men and women took the challenge to compete for the Biggest Loser title. The guys all weighed considerably more than three-hundred pounds; their guts were enormous. They were compelled to do outrageous amounts of exercise. I cannot describe how shocked I was when some of them lost no more than four pounds at the weekly weigh-in. That threw me off. I try and try to understand the physiology of weight loss, but I just can't seem to get it. I was sure those guys were going to make much more serious dents in their blubber, considering their girth and exercise regimen.

The contestants on *The Biggest Loser* look no less insane than our new patient. Aesthetically, it's a tossup who looks more mentally ill. Is it the poor soul who is plainly skin and bones? Or is it the poor souls who can barely navigate their mountains of flesh and fat?

And then there is Ellie, who isn't obviously skinny and isn't obviously obese. I am somewhere in the middle between these two extremes. I want to hold them fixed in my mind, lest I forget how bad it can be when madness rules the plate.

## *July 8th*

Just back from lunch. I ate an ostensibly innocent meal: chicken breast, tons of veggies, no bread, no sugar. But who am I kidding? I eat too much, too quickly and I am always in search of that *full* feeling.

I've got a problem with portion size, especially when I'm quite empty in my belly. I get this restless need to fill up at the next meal and when it comes around, my plate is a piled-up arrangement with lots of low-point foods. The portions are fit for a bruiser and usually invite some heckling from my family. Even though the foods I choose are ridiculously dietetic, everything all together is obviously an inordinate amount for one person.

The problem with meals of this nature is that I'm usually nauseous and burping within half an hour. They are the embodiment of the "your eyes are bigger than your stomach" phenomenon. My eyes devour the food and calculate the appropriate portion size. I am usually wrong and end up stuffing myself like a goose and washing it all down with too much Diet Cola. If this isn't a prescription for burping, I don't know what is.

This is insane because I know that I love how my body feels when I am not "stuffed to the gills," as Mom used to say.

One of the greatest treasures my mother left me was her turn of phrase. My mother had a way with words. She was articulate and impeccable with language. Her greatest power was her ability to speak and write.

In my early childhood, she used her words like a machete. In some cultures, people stun and kill their prey with poison arrows. Early Mom could have shown them a thing or two. She could slash and burn me with her precise enunciation of poison. Maybe my preoccupation with eating was an unconscious device to keep me from using my mouth so destructively, as she did.

Oddly enough, later Mom became demonstrably anorexic and truly hated eating meals. Dinners at my parents' were a bizarre *déjà vu*. There was my father begging her to eat at the very dining room table where, decades before, she had begged me to stop.

In her later years, my mom loved her nightly glass of vodka, straight up. This was the evening's entertainment that she shared with my father–a ritual they awaited daily with mutual anticipation. It was a single-glass arrangement, but a necessary pleasure, non-negotiable. Before and during the drink, Mom partook of *hors d'ouvres*. These *hors d'ouvres*–plus cookies, candy, ice creams and nuts–were truly all my mother wanted to eat during her last decade. She lost her taste for real food long before she died. Here and there she indulged in bits of these between-meal treasures. The nightly dinner was a sad affair; my poor father had no idea what sustained her on the planet, because she never ate much in front of him. She preferred her snacks on the sly.

Somehow the expression "stuffed to the gills" must have triggered these associations.

Something very powerful just dawned on me: *my* favorite foods are cookies, candy, ice cream and nuts. Holy moly, I never saw the connection before. What is this nonsense? Am I genetically predisposed to be her twin, craving the same foods as she? If you ask me my idea of gastronomic heaven, it's going to be the items above. I have to exclude the vodka, because I am too afraid of my predilection for addiction to even start a relationship with the bottle.

## *July 11$^{th}$*

Lately, I have been counting points, not calories. I never thought it would be my style, this Weight Watchers program that weighs me weekly and encourages me to keep my eating within a certain range. Believe me, if you play your cards right, you can eat handsome, nutritious meals and still stay perfectly legit. I went into the program full of piss and vinegar, hot to be the superstar. I was going to lose a ton in the first month.

But because I'm such a maniac, I am capable of scrounging around the kitchen for a snack not even ten minutes after a meal. Often, this happens when I feel I've been gypped on my points and the universe owes me more food. This is a delusion that I cannot be allowed if I want to be my best self.

Today, I ate a very mature, reasonable breakfast: my famous tuna and vegetables, a fresh salad with some bonus goodies, like a tablespoon of avocado and some sprinkles of parmesan cheese. To satisfy my need to crunch, I downed my low-point Swedish crackers. The point value of this meal was five in total.

Half an hour later, I was feeling kind of itchy for an extra point. I wasn't even hungry, yet I couldn't stop thinking like a crazy person about peanut butter. For a second, I told myself that I could play a little bit, savoring minute amounts of the glorious stuff. But who was I kidding? Minute amounts turn easily into shovelfuls. I got the jar off the table and stuck it in the back of the pantry.

I'm not always so disciplined. Lately, I might start out with an innocent health food cracker–good dietary fiber, no additives. A touch of butter and I'm in business. Usually, I escalate the activity to include a spoonful of peanut butter, a handful of seeds and raisins, a few slices of cheese... Then I start to think, why the hell not eat a cookie or two? Is it a crime? Have I no right to have a friendly, sweet treat? What's so bad about eating cookies? Why can't I eat cookies? I want to eat cookies!

I have on many occasions sworn off cookies entirely. I have enjoyed months of reprieve from sugar and white flour. While I have at times shed tears over the prospect of living without sweet confections, the truth is that in their absence I am perfectly capable of conducting myself like a grownup, one day at a time.

## *July 15th*

Well, I went on a five-day vacation to Holland and found myself back home two pounds up.

How did I do it, you ask? I had a gastronomic ball. Since I walked my feet off and pedaled like the devil on bike excursions, I figured I could eat all I wanted. I threw caution to the wind and indulged in the Dutch hobby: French fries smothered with mayonnaise.

One breakfast we had consisted of at least four slices of heavy health food bread and thick wedges of Gouda cheese. A different morning, when we took our breakfast in a restaurant, I ordered a fish salad. It sounded like a wise choice. They brought me a dish that looked more like mayonnaise salad than anything found in the ocean. You'd need a magnifying glass to find the fish.

I basically ate like my husband did. I didn't count calories, points, or carbohydrate grams. I was on vacation; I was living on the wild side, but not carrying on like a complete lunatic. So what the hell happened to me? How did I gain two pounds in five days? Is this a mystery or a logical consequence?

It is perfectly clear that I no more understand weight loss and gain than I understand air travel and telecommunication. People tell me that it's simple mathematics. It's never been simple for me.

It is nothing short of miraculous to change your body shape. A hairdo, I can understand. You cut hair, you curl it, you tease it, you dye it. These acts have clear and direct consequences on your mane. How a plate of pasta or a banana split gets broken down in my intestines, converted into essential nutrients and consequently flushed out, completely metamorphosed, is beyond me. Some people eat and eat and never put on an ounce, but the universe has always had other plans for me.

On the other hand, if I were one of those types who could eat huge quantities whenever and never look like it, I wouldn't have become a meditator or joined OA. It is because of this losing and gaining mystery that I embarked on my spiritual path.

I wanted the fat to disappear so I could look like a regular person in a bathing suit. A bathing suit has always been my standard. All my life, I've dreamed of marching around as easy as you please, at home in my body without a second or a hundredth thought. I never had the luxury of something so simple. When I see little kids playing, they seem completely impervious to the shapes of their bodies.

What would that have been like? What would it have been like to be me, looking lovely and graceful but not standing out? I developed a persona around the standout me. I created a self that was forever drawing attention to the fact that I was not only larger, but also better in every way imaginable. I became my own walking advertisement.

Did I do this because I weighed between twenty and fifty pounds more than I should have? Did I become the clown, the Earth Mother, the immodest and daring teenager, the most philanthropic and altruistic friend on the planet just to compensate for the fact that I was heavy? Who knows. It is possible that I had to invent a larger-than-life self, full of noise and passion, to keep you from holding my girth against me. I had to let you know I was amazing just in case my weight sidetracked you.

Because I suffered so much shame and embarrassment about being heavy, because I never understood why my tuna sandwiches ended up on my chin or thighs and yours didn't—because of all this, I turned to every conceivable philosophy, treatment and guru I could find. I have been on a quest for as long as I can remember. My frustration with overweight and food compulsion led me straight into the rooms of OA.

Before OA, I personally had never heard of anything so monumental psychologically as Step Four: "Made a searching and fearless moral inventory of ourselves." I took the challenge and plunged headlong into a searching and fearless moral inventory of myself. I thought a lot about the whole notion of morality, of goodness and badness. I tried to be courageous and look at things I had done that were not honest and fair. As I did this, I felt scared as hell that I was not as pristine a soul as I thought I was. I was lucky enough to have friends in the program who commiserated with me and supported my efforts to face the truth about myself.

Over the years, as I progressed in recovery, I was surprised to see how many insidious and stubborn little shreds of ugliness still clung to my character. I succeeded in getting rid of gross flaws while nevertheless sheathing myself in minute, microscopic con jobs, little white lies I shouldn't still have been telling.

You might not be aware of your weaknesses. You might vehemently object if they are pointed out to you. Stick around long enough in the program and you will come to know every nook and cranny of yourself, the good and the bad.

## July 27*th*

The other night, we made a birthday party for my youngest child. There is a fifty-pound divide between us. (She's my most petite child.)

A nice group of people enjoyed a tasty meal in a quaint Jerusalem restaurant. I have always savored Jerusalem at night. There is magic in the air. It is like no other place on the planet. If you're lucky enough to be near the Old City, your dinner may very well be accompanied by church bells, the *muezzin* call to prayer, or *yeshiva* boys reciting excerpts from the Torah.

I ate my meal and enjoyed it enormously. Everything was fine and within my point budget.

In the last half hour, when just a few of us remained, I began to eye some cheesecake. I saw the look on my husband's face when I said to him: "Give it over here, darling; I hardly ate my point quota for the day." The birthday girl, munching on forkfuls of chocolate cake at the other end of the table, said to me softly: "Why do you think you didn't get enough points? Didn't you eat the cream sauce on the salmon?"

I felt humiliated and became defensive and defiant. I told my husband *again* to send over the cheesecake. I didn't want any discussion. I was truly beginning to feel an irresistible urge to show the few remaining guests who the boss was.

I am sure that so many of my eating behaviors and the

feelings that support them are deeply rooted in spite. It's as if I am replaying ad nauseam the humiliations from my childhood, especially the ones in which my mom tried to rule my appetite. Just thinking that certain foods are off limits incenses me and makes me want them.

When I get so passionately locked into these patterns, I lose perspective. I've performed these actions for so long, they have become automatic and rigid.

My mother, in the early years, developed a set of facial expressions she used exclusively with me and my plate. They got more ferocious as the calorie count went up. She created a set of dirty looks to convey her disdain with my gobbling.

The more she scowled, the more I ate. She couldn't let up. I couldn't let up. We kept the monster alive.

Families of addicts often fall into this terrible trap of wanting "the best" for their loved ones. Who wants to watch someone he loves self-destruct in front of his eyes? It's maddening and everyone ends up feeling terrible. When families of alcoholics hide or destroy the bottles, they truly think they are saving a life.

When my own family cringes to witness an occasional public display of gobbling, I just want to eat more. But what *should* I expect of them? They know how tormented I am. They think they are helping me cope. They do not have a casual relationship with my overeating.

I cannot rewrite history, but I can say how sorry I am for what happened between my mother and me. It was a waste of time and energy. It put two fabulous women in a position significantly beneath them.

I can, however, affect the future. I don't have to

deliberately shovel inappropriate food down in the presence of my husband or children if I am particularly aggravated with them.

Today, I hereby pledge to make an effort to stay more conscious of what I am doing to myself and the ones I love. I don't want to upset my family. What joy can they possibly extract from watching me gorge myself when I should have reached satiation ages ago? It's a dumb, counter-productive power play. It helps no one.

You know something funny? After my husband reluctantly sent the cheesecake my way, I looked at it. I looked long and hard. It was a very fattening, elaborate affair. For one split second, I could have gone either way. I chose to put the fork down and allow sanity to reclaim its hold.

In that brief moment, I turned my fate around, temporarily, and decided on a glass of water. I let the whole situation go. I freed my husband. I let my daughter off the hook for noticing that I ate the cream sauce. What was she doing, counting my points for me? No, Ellie, idiot, she adores you and only wants you to succeed. Most of all, I liberated myself–at least this time–from falling into the trap of the I'll-show-you kind of eating that has ruled me since early childhood.

## *July 30th*

I had a perfectly successful day yesterday. I wrote for hours and conducted some marvelous family therapy and bio-feedback sessions. In the evening, I went to pay a condolence call.

For no reason that I can explain, I found myself

magnetized to the plentiful array of food. I began innocently with fruit. Then I got cute with too many pistachio nuts. I ate them very casually, ever aware of my husband's glance. I wasn't even hungry!

Knowing I would be weighed in the next day, what could I have been thinking? Why would I deliberately louse things up, especially when I am currently investigating my ancient pathology of defiant, in-your-face eating?

I've lost six pounds since June, even though I gained two in Holland. If I really want to get *somewhere*, I have to keep my wits about me and not take little forays as I did last night.

Thirty-five years ago, an editor at Harper and Row wrote that I seduced her with my writing. She loved my first manuscript, "The Possibility: A Study in Appearances and Disfigurement." When I came to New York to meet her, it was the morning after her apartment had been burglarized. She was noticeably distraught and impatient. The meeting was strained. We concluded that I would rewrite the introduction and send it to her.

I left her office in an absolute daze, got on a train at Grand Central, got off at my parents' station and promptly walked into a hair salon. I had my waist-length mane chopped off into a rather fashionable bob. When I got back to my parents' house, nobody could believe what I'd done, including me. It seemed to be the only way I could cope with the editor's vague request. I had no notion of what this gal actually wanted from me. I figured that if she was so taken by my writing, she would fix it herself as a gesture of respect. Being such a rookie writer, I didn't realize this was par for the course from an editor. I took it as a bad sign and acted out my frustration. I never contacted the editor again; I guess it was enough to get the invitation to make a meeting. I literally had no follow-through.

I remember the haircut. I'm probably forgetting the binge.

## *August 5th*

Driving to work the other day, knowing I was about to lead a group of addicts in one of our thrice-weekly sessions, I remembered I was going to Weight Watchers that night. I started to cry.

I decided that I would bring up the role of self-sabotage in our lives as a subject for discussion in the group. I would ask them to resonate to the sentence: "I keep disappointing myself and it just makes me weep."

The group jumped at the opportunity to speak; they were vying among themselves for a chance to be first to share. I let one fellow, who is normally reticent, open the experience. He began with a list of all his disappointments in life and how much sadness they caused him. I decided not to humiliate him by explaining that the topic was how much *he fails himself* and how miserable that makes him feel.

Instead, I thanked him for being brave enough to share. I then offered the stage to the other members of the group. Almost without exception, they addressed the theme of disappointment, neglecting to talk about the way they thwart their own efforts. Almost invariably, the group missed the point.

At the end of the session, I told them to listen to the assignment again and write about it for our next meeting.

They brought so much powerful material the next day, I thought I would faint from the depth of their honest self-reflections. It's not the kind of subject matter we usually have in a session. This approach gave them a chance to see their role as saboteurs in their own dramas.

## *August 6th*

I've been attending my Twelve-Step Overeaters Anonymous group every Friday for over two decades. It is, without a doubt, one of the highlights of my week. It's an all-female group, comprised of women I've known since the beginning. Naturally, new members join us now and then. But our core group is surprisingly faithful, showing up every week to give each other support.

"My girls," as I love to call them, are a magical mix of *mishegas*. We are sisters, only too knowledgeable about the pain and shame of addiction. The support in the room is holy. Love and tolerance shine between us. Everyone leaves an hour later changed a little because we were together.

I am happy to say that even though we initially joined OA because we were disgusted with our failures as dieters, overeating is rarely discussed. Spiritual challenges are almost exclusively the topic. What you'll hear in the room is either immense gratitude, or frustration at having failed to remember to live in partnership with the universe.

The other day was the first Friday of the month–when we read and write about that month's step at the meeting. August is the eighth month, so we had the privilege of going through Step Eight. It was my twenty-second time doing this.

Some anonymous writer, who was humble enough to

take no credit, wrote a breathtaking elaboration on the eighth step, explaining in detail what the step truly means on the deepest psycho-spiritual level. The writer explores the notion of harm, how we are all capable of causing pain to another human being through our acts or our prejudices.

At the meeting, I reveled in the notion of downsizing myself to such an extent that I could apologize sincerely for any wrongdoing. I couldn't wait for that juncture in the meeting when we get to choose a sentence from the writing and then put our own spin on it. I articulated my written apology for all the occasions on which I was a harsh and intolerant judge of mankind, on which I was loathsome, self-involved and neglectful, on which I was jealous and had critical thoughts.

I became possessed by the spirit of the step. I was boiling over with regret and remorse and I began to cry. I have always considered myself a good person, a do-gooder and righter of wrongs. But I am *far* from perfect and it took the Twelve Steps and many years to gradually foster a reliable awareness of myself.

When I arrived at my first ever meeting, part of me was screaming in my head: "Who needs this crap? I'm not gonna sit in a room with a group of jammed-up, neurotic overeaters." They were not in my league. They didn't know what I knew. After all, I'd been meditating over twenty years, I was a practicing psychologist... What did I have in common with these types?

"First of all," thought I, "what kind of nonsense is this, that I'm 'powerless over food,' as indicated in Step One? Who's powerless? What is it, heroin? Get real. I like to eat– it's not a drug. Let's not get carried away here. I can stop whenever I want. I've been on hundreds of diets. I am not obese. I may have thirty pounds to lose, but this does not qualify me as an addict. Give me a break. Maybe I'm powerless over my big fat appetite. But not even that–when I want to, I can always stop. I'm also nearing middle age and I've given birth to four children and I have bad eating habits and I don't exercise enough. And what is this part about sanity in Step Two?!"

The sanity business was the part that offended me most. How could anyone on earth describe *me* as insane? I'd always been madcap and a free spirit, but I had a totally balanced and reliable existence. I was the mother of four children, still in awe of my husband whom I'd adored for two decades, holding down a lecturing job at the Hebrew University for almost twenty years, plus innumerable other impressive accomplishments. Who, in God's name, would challenge my sanity?

In those early OA years, these kind of thoughts held me back from the rigorous self-examination that one must do in order to effectively get somewhere with the program.

You see, I thought I was sitting on top of the world. I figured overeating was my only problem. I dreamed of becoming slim, but I did not think that I had any other challenges. After all, I had accomplished so much in life already. I was a superstar.

While I was always quick to diagnose everybody else, I was slow to 'fess up to my own humanity.

As I saw it, I was one of the most balanced, happy, loving people on earth. Years ago, when I first started prescribing the Bach Flower Remedies, I thought that so many of them did not remotely apply to me. For instance, I was not critical and intolerant, though it was an apt description of an acquaintance of mine. *She* was impossible and scathing in her relentless badgering. *She* had a comment on everything and everybody. I cringed when I was near her. She needed that remedy–and certainly, I was nothing like her!

It took years to recognize to what degree I too had some of the same features. What a rude awakening. What a shameful discovery. As I put down the food and the vomiting, I started to hear my inner voice. I started to notice what a nasty little critic I could be. It was a rather snotty superiority that I possessed and it embarrasses me to even mention it now.

My mother's favorite pastime was to catch people's inconsistencies, lies, and misrepresentations. She was like a Venus flytrap, a gorgeous carnivorous flower. She was relentless with her prey and ended up sparring almost every time we met. You could tell she loved doing this. In the old days, she was always sniffing around for gaping holes in my stories. Her idea of a fun afternoon was catching the discrepancies in my tales. I always had a tendency to hyperbolize and catastrophize. I made minor events into gala celebrations, painting my own version of things. I played to my audience; if I wanted sympathy or shock value, I could pull them out of a hat. As embarrassing as it is to say, I liked attention and knew how to get it.

It wasn't until after years of meditation that Ev was mellowed enough to let go of being right. The truth is, over time, she really began to discover her true nature and purpose. The later Ev was the greater Ev.

Today, when I catch myself trying to catch other people, delightedly pointing out their frailties in my comical and superior manner, I have to get the hook and yank myself off the stage. Otherwise I'd be foaming at the mouth till dawn, pointing out all their inconsistencies like Ev did.

I tend to stick my nose into other people's business. As a psychologist, this is expected of me. As a parent, I am told that it is an absolute necessity. The question I raise here is: To what degree should I be involved in other people's lives?

I can recall a time, long ago, when I was sitting in a restaurant, having lunch with my dear friend Alfredo. At some point in the conversation, I collapsed into tears and wept about how frustrated I was with my figure. My friend is a tennis pro, a stand-up comedian and wise man all rolled into a body that looks like a greyhound with curls. He is very compassionate and funny as hell. He comforted me as I poured out my heartache.

After this cathartic, soul-baring scene, I looked up and saw a refrigerator displaying some obscene desserts. I begged his forgiveness, apologizing profusely (like a true addict) and swearing that this was the last time I would order a chocolate mousse cake.

We still laugh about it. But you know the funny thing? I knew I was going to my first OA meeting that night and somewhere, in the back of my mind, I truly believed I was having a farewell party.

As I recall the dramatic scene I had with Al, I feel I must thank him publicly for not doing what *I* might have done if the tables were turned. He did not roll his eyes. He did not give me a lecture on my inconsistencies. He did not humiliate me. He just laughed with me.

Alfredo could have had a field day with my one minute weeping, one minute gobbling, but he let it alone. He was wise enough to know that trying to stop me would only make me defensive. This was my arena of insanity. He was not over-engaged in my *mishegas*. He had enough of his own that he did not want me trampling on.

That judgmental voice inside has no humility.

It can only exist if I refuse to own the fact that I am as flawed as anyone else in my midst.

Until I did the fourth step for the first time–making a fearless and searching moral inventory of myself–I did not realize that one of my major character defects was laziness. God forgive me, but what else could I call myself when I sometimes hoped to be temporarily gravely ill, sick enough to lose my appetite and get skinny without having to fight food cravings?

There is a pretty-faced young woman with whom I work. She is short and was rather fat until a few months ago, when she had a gastric bypass; she has by now lost sixty pounds. It's hard for me not to be acutely jealous. I don't want surgery, but I do want weight loss. Sometimes I have fantasies that I will have the doctor Hoover my whole body.

What an eye-opener!

For years, I believed that all I had to do was lose weight. OA has taught me that I have to lose some of my more childish character defects. This experiment might ostensibly look like a journey into weight loss, but please do not be mistaken. The weight I hope to lose is more about who I am, rather than what I look like.

## *August 8th*

The Big Book of AA says that addicts are "restless, irritable and discontent." I would do anything to get away from adjectives of this nature. I know these traits, especially the restlessness, all too well. More often than I would like, I am *nudgy* and bored. From a place of restlessness, it's easy to become irritable and discontented. In such moments, I definitely gravitate toward overeating and TV. They're my pacifier, my outlet.

I recall various times when I have been settling in for a cozy evening in front of the TV and have remembered a little peanut butter left in the jar, or some little dessert that I have been saving. I sneak past Michael, who is probably watching the news in Hebrew; I hope he doesn't see me and beckon for me to join him.

There's a kind of ritual we have in the evenings after we finish our days' commitments. He goes to his study to recline and watch his TV shows while I retreat to our bed to read or gaze at my more idiotic programs in English. After the kind of hugely exhausting days he puts in, often staying on his feet for hours at a time, he wants to watch science and politics. I respect that about him, but I don't want to lie in the crook of his arm hearing Israeli Knesset members duke it out over the best strategy for dealing with the Hezbollah. Frankly, I'd rather watch a good, crappy American soap opera.

Sometimes, when I turn down the chance to join him, I just want to go to bed. Other times, something in of the tone of my "Not now, darling," makes us both acutely aware that I am on a quest for some serious eating. The thought of dessert is small potatoes compared to the kind of nonsense I may be surreptitiously cooking up. On the nights when I am particularly restless, I need a lot more than re-runs of *Homeland* to carry me through till we retire for bed. I frequent the kitchen, the storehouse of my more pathetic coping strategies.

In the end, Michael finds me propped up in bed somewhere between intoxication and unconsciousness, barely able to keep my eyes open. What may begin with a teaspoon of peanut butter likely ends up compromised with the choice of a hefty portion of granola and 0% yoghurt. I may choose the granola because it is so nutritious and crunchy and because the chewing requirements are greater–maybe enough time will elapse between the onset and the completion to give my stomach a chance to register its fullness.

No such luck. By the time such a party is over, I have consumed enough carbohydrates to make me sleepy and dull-witted.

How many problems in life have I looked at and decided, instinctively, to solve with food? I don't think I've uncovered all of them yet.

## *August 11th*

I have a new little game going on that I think of as my "quick feeds." These are the little escapades that take place when my hand hastily grabs and shoves "a little something" into my mouth. I don't calculate the point value of these speed munches. I tend to think that they don't count. In my magical thinking, that which is eaten quickly, while standing, doesn't register as food or calories.

I have a bar of bittersweet, sugar-free chocolate nestled in the freezer under a bag of pita. On occasion, when I'm getting some ice for the Diet Cola (which I'm back to drinking), my hand will accidentally finger the chocolate. Often I snap off a piece and shove it in my mouth. At that point, I will have a fit of temporary amnesia and conveniently forget to record the event.

It's all about honesty. When I pretend that things are not as they really are, do I figure I can get away with this? Most people think they can. Addicts are especially given to this kind of thinking. They try to pull the wool over everyone's eyes and lie to themselves. If you want to see self-deception in its most foul form, watch an addict–it's horrifying.

I do know that there is no real way to cheat, to tiptoe past my metabolism and keep my weight stable. My father always said: "You can't fool your body." If you eat more than your body can burn, you will gain weight. The only way to cheat that system is by purging, and I have been spared from that little piece of pathology for years. Thank you, universe!

Want to know a secret? I wouldn't have much respect for a higher power that let me get away with murder, pretending not to notice my scam.

I know only too well how hard it is to lose weight at this stage of the game. Twenty pounds (my first benchmark goal) was a six-week gig in the old days. Not anymore, friends. I'm only at eight.

Because I am such a carnivore and connoisseur of the richest, fattiest items on the planet, it's usually fun on a protein diet for the first few weeks. And that's the thing of it; I never, except for that one bad period, ever let myself get so obese that a few serious weeks without carbs wouldn't straighten me out.

This summer, my last summer as a fat girl, I need a different strategy. Even if I could go to the Himalayas for two months, subsisting on berries and roots, it still might not be enough. I have to look at this from an entirely different angle. I need a lifestyle change, a plan that will carry me through the long haul. Drastic diets for me are a guarantee of ultimate failure.

The other day, staring at my reflection in a shop window, I imagined standing in that same spot a year from now. I will don my white sleeveless cotton jersey top and light khaki trousers. I love this look. I want this look.

Maybe it's better that I don't know how big my rear-end looks in my khaki trousers these days. Maybe it's better that I don't know how heavy my arms look. I am blissfully unaware, so I march around feeling like a good-looking middle-aged powerhouse and thank God I don't have eyes in the back of my head.

## *August 13th*

This date has been engraved in my heart for fifteen years. On that day, I was in a hotel in Manhattan. It was the afternoon; we were getting ready for my darling niece Hilary's wedding. I had rented four rooms in the hotel. My father dared me to foot the bill and I welcomed the opportunity. Somehow, it's all his money anyway. But that's not the point. My mom didn't feel well and it just so happened that a friend of mine, a physician from China, was staying at a hotel nearby. He came over and gave my mother a checkup. Her heart was terribly weak by then, but she managed to rise to the occasion. She wasn't going to miss her first grandchild's wedding.

We all got there, pushing away any anxiety we had

about my mom's health. Three of my four children attended. Formal dress was required. What a sight we were, tottering on high heels in our evening gowns and tuxedoes. Two of my children even flew in from a trip to India in order to partake in the festivities. Because it was such a different kind of day, it fixed itself into my calendar memory.

It was to be the last August 13th of my mother's life. It was to be the last time we all gathered together like that to celebrate. By the winter, we gathered to mourn her.

## *August 15th*

Partially because I have always been somewhat sedentary, I have developed a private set of belief systems and prejudices against sports. The other day, I caught myself at an OA meeting reacting, internally of course, in a rather abrasive manner when I heard someone lament not being able to go for her morning swim.

I looked at her, a tiny, energetic woman, and felt scorn rising up within me. I said to myself, "She must be an exercise bulimic–she's not fooling me. She must have a whole elaborate routine worked out. She must be terrified to eat, fearing that she will put on weight."

This lady's exercising triggered my internal critic, a smokescreen for my real feelings of jealousy. She can move her body with glee and I must struggle to ride a bike for forty minutes (yep–I'm up to forty!). I am just plain envious that someone can get past all that heart pounding and sweating and find the experience pleasurable.

I take after my mother's side of the family; none of them ever moved. I don't recall ever going on a walk with my mom. She was all brain. She had a body; she just didn't move it. She did, however, have it massaged. Weekly, some lady would come over with a portable massage table. That was her idea of heaven.

My dad, bless his soul, had a crappy exercise bicycle that he rode till the last ten days of his life. He was ninety-one years old and took this activity seriously. Until his later years, he walked and sat with dignity. His posture was always impressive. He had strength in his arms like a young athlete.

Growing up, some of my friends had parents who skied or played tennis. Just thinking about my parents doing any of that makes me roar with laughter. My dad did play golf. He had all kinds of golf outfits. It was a bone of contention in their marriage. My mother resented his weekly forays onto the green.

I vaguely recall that my brother wanted to take me skiing when I was in tenth grade. The trip fell through and the subject never came up again. The closest I got to skiing was buying stretch pants and a powder-blue ski parka, which remained a permanent resident of my closet till I got married and moved away.

Both of my parents were in agreement on one aspect of physical activity–people who treat athletics like a meaningful pursuit (my dad's forays didn't count) are moronic.

## *August 18th*

Here's a curious phenomenon–it's called the three-breakfast Ellie. It goes something like this: I get up earlier than everybody else on Saturday morning. I'm hungry. I go into the kitchen and rustle up a sensible, focused, light meal.

Breakfast number one, eaten at 8 a.m.: a tasty, juicy orange with cottage cheese. This repast could hold me. It's nutritious and tasty, yet modest. I am very pleased. After all, with a three-point breakfast, I have lots of room for treats, don't I?

Breakfast number two, 9:30 a.m.: Friends drop by for a spontaneous brunch. At this meal, I sit down with them so we can eat together. They are all slim, sophisticated Israelis who want to share some classy bread and French cheese with me. The bread, I decline; the cheese is another matter. The fact that the percentage of fat is forty-three doesn't seem to bother the company, so why should it bother me?

Breakfast number three, 11 a.m.: An exaggerated bowl of my favorite cereal, Grape Nuts. Everyone else is eating and I want to be sociable. I tell myself that if I eat this, I will most likely forgo lunch. I know, of course, that I'm only fooling myself again.

By noon, on a given Saturday, I have already eaten three breakfasts and jacked up my points for the day.

Mind you, it could even just be tomatoes and carrots for breakfast number two–friendly little no-pointers. Once I stretch my stomach out, filling myself to the brim, I'm screwed. Once I've had my fill, I start to get dangerous and become a predator.

I want to go into the notion of "filling myself to the brim." I have often been astounded by this need and ability of mine. I've seen other people do it too. There's a certain kind of food you want to fill up on and it's decidedly not salad. It veers towards starchy fare: potatoes, rice, bread. A hot, cooked meal.

I don't *always* want to do this. Truly, I don't. There are

times when I feel just fine with an apple or a carrot and don't crave the likes of a huge he-man's meal. Other times, there are not enough cookies in the neighborhood to sate my unquenchable appetite.

There was a time when I developed a very close personal bond with breadsticks. I want to describe them, because they are not remotely like the ones I knew that they served in Italy or in Italian restaurants in Manhattan. First of all, they are huge, almost the size of a drum major's baton. They are invariably covered in sesame. They are not the delicate, airy affairs that come in packages of two; they are husky, crunchy stinkers and they taunt me. I don't do well knowing they are being kept fresh in a box in the kitchen.

My current little nemesis is Grape Nuts. Damn it, I measure myself out a quarter of a cup at a time, but I still see a reliance on it. It has escalated beyond mealtime and metamorphosed into a snack. I justify eating it because it is so good for my digestion.

Come on, Ellie. You know better than that.

## *August 20th*

This morning, I caught a glimpse of myself in a mirror. I was not pleased. In fact, I felt disheartened and overwhelmed. I feel remorse for too many years of neglect, overindulgence and escape.

You see, it's very tricky. Eating is something everyone does several times a day. I am not doing something extraordinary and bizarre. I do not have, God forbid, a secret room in which I hide away from the world and eat sticky buns. I eat the same meals as my dining partners. Unfortunately, I do not end up looking like everyone else.

I remember my first pregnancy. At that time, one could not get "everything American" in Israel. Imported items and ideas were still late in coming. Health food stores were scarce; baked goods were more often created at home than found on the shelves.

My husband and I were still newlyweds, recent immigrants, and had plenty of free time. When I passed the period of morning sickness, I discovered the real meaning of food cravings. I might note here that I was rather slim and had actually maintained my weight from the big diet five years before.

With no children yet and no formal jobs in place, we were a couple of free birds who loved discovering the treasures of Israel on our own. Jerusalem's Old City was a safe and exotic place back then. We were frequent visitors.

When I felt the urge for spaghetti Bolognese, we knew where to find it. We had a pal named Gino who just loved cooking it for me. When I couldn't live without rare roast beef–a rarity in Israel–we found two sources. Chinese restaurants were in short supply, but we managed to score a few decent egg rolls while my first-born was *in utero*.

The New Yorker in me loved going out to eat. For most Israelis, dining out was an infrequent treat. In my repertoire, it was an everyday occurrence.

It was funny. For the first time in my life I became aware of distinct food cravings. While I did develop a taste for freaky combinations, it was never the traditional pickles and ice cream.

Many of those meals never got digested, if you know what I mean. It was the most obvious and logical thing I could do to get relief. By my fifth month of pregnancy, I was slim and radiant. I had a lot of energy and my mood was sublime.

The night I went to give birth, I had a mad craving for rack of lamb and mint jelly sauce, specifically from the old Hilton hotel. Barefoot, I sat in the lotus position and gobbled down charbroiled lamb. The contrast with the sweet jelly was divine. My doctor was horrified when that pink-and-green stuff wound up all over my hospital gown during the delivery.

I took the matter of purging very casually during all my pregnancies. It would never have dawned on me to use it as a diet strategy; I simply felt stuffed and took the necessary steps to ease my discomfort. I did not regard this as a bulimic activity. I did it in a completely reasonable manner. I figured it came with the territory of pregnancy.

Things started to get out of hand after my fourth child was born. Because I was so successful at self-deception, I did not worry about what was going on. I thought I was surely smart and sane. I thought I was doing myself a favor, being friendly to my body with this early evacuation of potentially hazardous material.

After a wildly strenuous food festival of all the tasty items you could imagine, I would announce openly that I was going to straighten myself out. I hastened to add: "I'll be back for dessert." Nobody raised an eyebrow. Maybe they thought I was kidding. I certainly didn't have the body type expected of a bulimic; for ten years of this nonsense, my weight fluctuated, but I was mostly plump. Still, to this day, it baffles me that not once did anybody comment or try to stop me.

I did it in restaurants, other peoples' homes–wherever, whenever. I recall telling my friend Nachi that I occasionally binged and purged on purpose. He was frankly horrified. He told me to stop it and not be afraid if I put on a lot of weight ("Fat chance," I thought). He said my daughters would soon be approaching adolescence and that this food behavior would be a dangerous example for them. The part about my daughters did scare me into stopping for several years. I don't know how I was able to do it just like that. It was as if my friend's influence on me was so great that it inexplicably removed the obsession. I might add here that he was my first official hypnosis teacher.

I cannot recall exactly what led me back to the madness, but some of my wildest binge and purge behaviors took place when I began OA.

In my early days with the program, I did everything by the book: I attended three meetings a week, found a sponsor, spoke to her daily and followed a food plan. I was a diligent student of the Twelve Steps; I was serious and chomping at the bit to do things the right way. My weight went down and I felt I had been embraced by the sanest, most spiritual system I had ever encountered.

The sponsor I took was a nice Israeli lady I saw at my first meeting. Following the rules precisely, I called her in the mornings and read out loud from the writing assignment of the day. These were always connected to my overeating and the emotions behind it. I had to search my soul, honestly and bravely, to come up with flaws in my character. She patiently supported me through the first seven steps. She was my introduction to this very fabulous journey.

The first time I screwed up, I felt like a sinner. I had somehow ended up standing in front of the refrigerator and eating five huge cookies that I had bought for my children. It took me no time at all to gobble them down. The cookies were frozen. That didn't bother me; I was in a trance, not in my right mind. Minutes later, I had already washed down the crime scene with a liter of water. The guilt and the hastiness of the ingestion quickly made me feel sick to my stomach. Carrying so much shame on my shoulders, I found myself on my knees in front of the toilet.

I felt pathological. I embarrassed myself. Here I was in the program, reading the literature and using the tools, and yet I was up to my eyeballs in food insanity again. I was scared, but I did not disclose my secret. For a year, I thought of myself as a model Twelve-Stepper, slim and lovely, who walked the talk. But I was also a crazy lady with a sneaky food disorder.

On a trip I took with my husband to Thailand during my first year in OA, the food was out of this world. The fruits and baked goods were divine. The hotel catered to an international crowd, so the tables were piled high with every conceivable tasty treat on the planet. I'd excuse myself–again to no raised eyebrows–twice during a buffet breakfast meal.

Let's face it, I wasn't exactly sitting in our hotel room lost in a binge and purge ritual. Because it was a trip, I gave myself license to party. When I got home, I went back to my Twelve Steps and continued on my merry way.

About six months later, I took my parents to Florida to visit their respective siblings. I was in great shape, deeply into the Twelve Steps and very proud.

On the first night, I raided the hotel mini-bar. I couldn't believe what I had done. Horrified, I rushed to the toilet to straighten things out. I hadn't done anything like this in quite a while, nor had I binged. "Whoops," I thought, "where is this coming from? Better stop and forgive myself."

The next night, my parents treated the extended family to a big celebration at a restaurant. Everyone was there, all my cousins, aunts and uncles. There was even another generation of young people–my cousins' children. Many of these cousins were rather heavy. I felt like a star, slender and successful. My parents were proud and my father was bragging about his daughter the doctor.

At dessert time, I began cruising the fancy cakes. The relatives were eating with abandon and looked it. I figured, "I'll have some of that myself."

I went from lemon meringue to key lime pie in nothing flat. When I hit the devil's food cake, my father placed his hand on mine and said: "Darling, I think you've had enough." I didn't respond or flare up. I put my fork down. But I sure didn't fancy the interruption–nobody comes between me and my food.

The ever-courteous hotel staff had replenished my candy supply when I got back to the hotel. I hit the mini-bar before I even turned on the TV.

With all these slips and digressions, I still figured I was basically living an abstinent life. Not once did it dawn on me that I needed a guide out of the intermittent bulimia.

Things didn't change until my first birthday as a Twelve-Stepper, when my sponsor moved to America. I needed someone to work Steps Eight through Twelve with me. In the fall, feeling like a poster girl for the program, I went to an unusually large OA meeting. There were people in the room that I had never seen before. I set my eyes on a gal who looked remarkably like Princess Diana–something about her complexion, coloring, hairdo and eyes. She gave a brief talk about her disease and recovery. It sounded impressive.

OA literature recommends you find a sponsor who seems to have what you want (spiritually, physically and emotionally) and ask her how she achieved it; I asked Helen if she would consider becoming my sponsor. She agreed.

With both of us being American, we established a different chemistry from the start. I felt more comfortable with her than I had with the other woman I had worked with; maybe something about having to speak Hebrew had stifled me and kept my relationship with her very formal and proper. With Helen, things were different. She encouraged me to call her when I felt shaky, either with my food or my emotions.

A very unusual bond can exist between a sponsor and a protégée. It is a unique relationship. We didn't start out as friends, but rather as two individuals engaged in a purely psychological and spiritual dialogue. Within this framework, she generously volunteered her time and wisdom to me as I struggled with my issues. I was encouraged to speak every day to a non-judgmental, successfully abstinent human being who was dedicated to my personal recovery from my insidious disease. I do not know of anything, other than Twelve-Step programs, that supports such a lofty ideal as this.

With Helen as my sponsor, coach, mentor, and

guardian angel, we began daily phone calls in which I read my written assignments to her. We also discussed my food plan: complete abstinence from sugar, white flour and general overeating.

One morning, as fate would have it, I slipped and found myself at a little bulimia party. I rushed to call my darling sponsor. I told her what I ate, how I ate it and how I wrapped up the whole affair in the toilet.

"You did what?" she said.

"I ate like a maniac, I told you."

"Did you say you vomited?"

"Yeah, so what? I do it all the time; wait, I don't mean I do it all the time, but I do it whenever, if I've eaten too much, you know?"

"Ellie, are you listening to yourself?"

"What are you making such a big deal about? I am not exactly bulimic now, am I?" I answered.

She told me she didn't care if I gained fifty pounds. I could not, absolutely not, ever entertain the idea of behaving like this again.

I did not like her butting in. She had overstepped her bounds. Can you believe it? I actually thought she had a nerve, playing psychologist. That was my role, not hers.

I felt indignant. It was my first self-disclosure of this nature in OA and I felt raw, exposed. Thank God, the program is anonymous. I was mortified at the idea of anyone thinking of me as bulimic. I was frightened that people would think that *this* was my weight-loss secret, rather than all my hard-won abstinence.

A few weeks after this sponsorial intervention, I traveled to America to visit my parents. Sunday morning, my father held court on the back porch, reclining on a white, wrought-iron chaise lounge that he loved. With his eyes closed, he launched into a monologue about his relationship with the universe. He seemed to feel that the time was right to share his most private thoughts on the meaning of his life.

These kinds of lectures were not exactly my mother's favorite thing. Her pursed lips screamed, "Not *you* telling us again about God." We aggravated her when we played Ellie-sitting-at-the guru's-feet. The truth is, though, she was no less a mentor in her way. My parents were just stylistically polar opposites.

The sermon ended with: "You know, my child, I have always considered myself a servant of the Lord."

Hearing my father describe himself in this way thrilled me. I had never realized, till I heard the thought articulated, that I was serving the Lord too. Wasn't it true that I lived to serve the greater good? Didn't I rush to help people before they needed to humiliate themselves and ask for it? Didn't I shower people with love and bundle them up with compliments and heartfelt affirmations?

After this big moment with my dad, I concretized this view of myself–I was in a partnership with the Almighty. My business cards could have said: Dr. Ellie, Servant of the Lord.

A few days after this remarkable awakening, I overate. I guess I forgot that I was supposed to be a servant of the Lord. I temporarily switched loyalties to the service of the hungry beast within, leaving my insights at the front door of the restaurant I went to with my parents. I like to whoop it up in American restaurants, eating foods from my childhood. I had a tasty grilled cheese sandwich and French fries, washed down with a big glass of Diet Coke. I figured I'd go take care of this gastronomic festival before I settled down to a nice hot apple pie à la mode for dessert.

But I found I couldn't do it. I tried; it just didn't happen. I wasn't able to physically manifest the act.

By the grace of God, I have never resorted to doing anything this insane with my food again. It was miraculously lifted out of my repertoire. I have no logical explanation for this; the only way I can possibly understand it is to see it as a consequence of that talk with my father. It is a present I treasure. It is forever on my gratitude list. I am never blasé about it. I did not have to bite the bullet, nor did I have to make a teeth-clenching effort. It just happened.

I call this, my reprieve from bulimia, my OA gift. The foundation of the program is spiritual in nature and by the time you reach Step Twelve, you are supposed to have had an awakening of sorts. Miracles abound and you finally realize that a higher power is doing for you what you could not do for yourself. Thousands of people have experienced such revolutionary changes.

This was a difficult aspect of the program for me. I've always had a funky relationship with my spirituality. The only prayers I consent to utter are thank-yous and expressions of awe. I adamantly refuse to pray for favors.

In prayers and supplications, people beg a higher power for what they want. I find this distasteful and audacious. Since this higher power is supposed to be omniscient and omnipotent, who am I to be giving orders? All I have to do is the right thing.

Not all prayers are answered; who doesn't know that? But what dictates that this child's innocent prayer be answered and this man's devoutly performed prayer go unheard and unheeded? Do you have to be a certain religion to have your prayer answered? Do you need to wash your hands or perform some worthy-making ritual before prayer?

I do think the act of prayer and the sincerity of intention have value in themselves. Merely formulating what you want to be free from is already rather liberating. Specifying what you would like to be brave enough to undertake is plenty empowering.

(My older daughter tells me that if I am in a funk, I should grab God by His beard and demand: "Get over here, I need You now. You let me get into this mess, so You get me out of it, right now. Right now, I say."

She is a feisty one. She is my resident prayer warrior. She is not embarrassed to make demands; she thinks nothing of letting God know she needs Him NOW. Next to her I feel like I'm just tiptoeing around, ashamed to be bossy or demanding about my needs. Is it because of faith or fear that I don't dare make a big fuss, that I play it safe?)

At the time of this divine intervention, my reprieve from bulimia, I hadn't even completely finished the Steps. The divine shone a light on me early in my program. I was free at last from the pathology of purging. Hallelujah! How wonderful that my father was the agent of this miracle. How lucky I am that someone so wise happened to be my father.

While I know there's a long road ahead of me, I must not be afraid to march on with clear goals in mind. It's not hard to conjure up my father; in fact, it's one of my daily requirements. I am very fortunate to have been the daughter of someone so spiritually gifted.

## *August 23rd*

A few days ago I was watching a British film on clutter. (I tend to fancy psychologically-oriented documentaries.) The clutterer was a middle-aged woman who had lost her husband about ten years before. He was a physician and she was his sidekick, wife and mother of his brood. Throughout the program, we got a glimpse into the lives of this remarkably lovely twosome, who chose to reside in remote places so he could tend to the sick and poor.

The early segment of the documentary was shot in the 1970s. These two looked like an advertisement for flower children, long-haired and skinny as rats. They were dressed in loud floral prints and they both wore boots with fringes. In one scene, she played a guitar and gazed at her husband as if he were a god.

By the latter part of the film, she had turned into one of the fattest women I have ever seen in my life. Her gross overweight was *never* addressed. The only subject at hand was her need to hold on to her keepsakes, a clinging to her past that was expressed through the metaphor of hoarding. She was unable to part with mountains of clutter. I looked on in awe. How did she get that way?

I understood this lady's pain. I guess losing her husband left her with a gaping hole of emptiness. The best she could do was to fill it with food and clutter.

When *I* cannot bear my painful emotions and complicated ruminations, *I* always run to put something in my mouth. It is the easiest, most obvious thing to do. From the first day of my existence, I have always felt calmer with something in my mouth.

I can't believe it's taken me so long to recognize this. It is so plainly a fundamental aspect of my life. Stuffing down, gorging, is a technique designed to keep emotions at bay and ensure that I am stoned enough on sugar and flour to stay light and cheery.

What a complex thing the mind is. Seeing a program about someone who has eaten themselves close to death upsets me so much that I want to eat to comfort myself from these profoundly pained emotions (that someone *else* must be feeling).

I yearn to help the doctor's wife. She reminds me of another morbidly obese woman I saw once in a movie. The mother in *What's Eating Gilbert Grape?* has lost her husband and has subsequently completely lost herself to food consumption, cigarette smoking and the very subtle sport of pressing a remote control to flip the channels. The few times we see her walk across the room, the floorboards shake. She is barely alive. She has become a monstrosity, the object of the town's gawking gaze.

This obese woman, six-hundred pounds at least, whose every step reverberates like a thunderclap, is my worst nightmare. She is what could happen if I let go, tumbling onto piles of food, losing all sense of proportion, giving up.

She breaks my heart up there, dominating the screen. Her arms and legs are inhuman. There is a scene in the film in which we see a photograph of her, years before–an absolutely lovely woman, thin and beautiful, just like the lady in the documentary on clutter. There is no hint of the perversity that's coming.

They are not my heroes, but we are kindred spirits. I know too well how they let themselves go.

## *August 26$^{nd}$*

At any point in my history as a fat girl, there have been numbers to represent success or desperate failure.

My relationship with the scale is disconcerting. If I weigh less than expected, instead of flowing with the momentum, I invariably screw up my progress and give myself license to overeat. If I haven't lost as much as I hoped for, the only way I know how to soothe myself is by chewing and swallowing. So, naturally, I want to turn to food in order to comfort myself for being heavy. Crazy, crazy thinking. I weave the web and trap myself in it.

In this particular arena, both success and failure intimidate me. The result is the same.

I am exposed and raw, my skin is thin. Sometimes it feels that I am without any defenses. I can be knocked over by things within me—memories, resentments and fears. I can lose sleep over things that do not affect me directly. I find myself looking up at the sky and wondering why my beloved Creator lets terrible things happen. Rejection and humiliation upset me, often when they have absolutely nothing to do with me. Mental illness and physical illness make me weep. I am beside myself when I see what harm people cause themselves and others.

And then I have to live with *my* stuff—my self-loathing and ruthless demands for perfection, my swinging moods that aren't easily harnessed, my aging body that often fails me, and the big and little disappointments and setbacks that come my way.

When I was a child, something went terribly wrong in my life. There is no question that the eye trauma took a toll. The incident in Bermuda really loused me up. My ridiculous growth spurt didn't help either. Add shame and ridicule to this potpourri.

I was prepared to cut myself off completely from any of these emotional states. Early in my childhood, I took a metaphorical chainsaw and chopped off my head. I kept it at a safe distance from my heart, just enough to make sure I didn't know how I was feeling. Food kept me comfortably numb.

Even though I've risen from the ashes of my childhood, frequently reinventing myself, I still *schlep* an emotional hunchback.

I no longer eat because of the eye operation or Bermuda. I eat to cope with the existential travesty, with big global things and little household nuisances. I've graduated to a whole other level of reasons.

This part of me rears its head when I can't handle my emotions. She chooses hunger instead of feeling pain. It is more tolerable to her to experience appetite than to feel confusion, anger or sadness.

I remember Twelve-Step guru Judi Hollis saying something like: There should be nothing you eat, drink or buy to "make a difference." If you think that something can *do it* for you, beware. For addictive thinkers, IT is being pursued hotly in the hopes that it will *help* them somehow. Addicts use their addictions to temper their existential angst.

I eat for comfort, and to show others who is boss, and for so many other reasons too numerous to list. When these are not factored in, I fail to understand why it takes me so long to lose weight. I look at the scale, I look at the calendar and I'm dumbfounded. How come I've been gaining, not losing? I should be asking, "God, when am I going to be able to make peace with the hard stuff?"

I am larger than life, brilliant and daring, yet I am handicapped. Something is keeping me from getting it all together; little remnants of my past form enormous obstacles. I have come a long way, but I have failed to get spiritually high enough for my taste. I still have a restless and critical mind. Even after decades of daily meditation, I like to gossip and point other people's weaknesses for my own jollies, pretending that it is for their own good and that I get nothing out of it.

I've helped so many of people. Between my patients and my students, hundreds have been inspired by me; many have stayed in touch with me over the years and are proud to share how their lives have turned around. I have seen them blossom in response to our work together. But deep inside my soul, something stinky keeps me from refining my nature to impeccability.

I want to shed the weight of distorted thinking. It would be a dream to look normal in a skimpy summer dress, of course, but I want more than that. I want my spirit to exude lightness. I want freedom from all the pain that weighs me down and shackles my soul.

With each pound I lose–and I have lost several by now–I pray to gain a pound of courage, stability, faith, modesty, maturity and humility.

I am impatient to be well again. I am chomping at the bit to experience the new me. It will take a good year till we get to next summer. In this year I hope to shed a lot more than fifty pounds. I hope to shed every piece of crap that has taken up residence inside of me. I am shooting for the moon. I want this journey to bring me peace.

This is the diet for my soul. This is the hardest thing I have ever done in my life. For every pound of fat I lose, I hope I lose tons of the tenacious flaws that have weighed me down.

I thought I was doing the Twelve Steps to the best of my ability over these last years. I never knew why I didn't especially get anywhere. Today, by the grace of God, the debris from a lifetime of spiritual shenanigans is clearing and a new me is begging for oxygen.

Today, I am committing to be much more conscious. Just because I don't like my emotions doesn't mean I need to deny or douse them with food. When I realize I am jealous, I must *look* at this feeling. When I feel threatened, I must look the emotion in the face and see what I can do about it.

No kidding, but stuffing my face has never been a good solution to anything in my life.

## *August 27$^{rd}$*

For all the progress I've been making with my self-examination lately, having a jerky addiction still means that I may have to spend the rest of my days being vigilant. My instincts, thought patterns and everyday routines are the product of decades. It will take no little time to break them down and break away from them.

Just this morning, for example, I got too friendly with some tasty whole grain bread. Since I was only eating a salad, I thought, "Why not enjoy some extra points?" Curious to know the full extent of this caper, I went back to the table afterward and took a slice of bread off a guest's plate with an apologetic look that was intended to convey the sentiment, "Forgive me, I am a mental case, a compulsive overeater, who is doing penance and is trying to make up for lost time." I marched over to my food scale and received shocking news: I had just shoveled down one hundred and fifty grams of bread that I surely didn't need. I had ingested way too many points and I had hardly started the day.

I seem to recall a rumor that bread is love. What the hell does that mean? If I am looking for love, I'd rather eat chocolate.

I need to stop comparing myself with the general atmosphere, wondering whether I'm thinner or fatter than the humanity around me. If I'm in public, I feel like I owe some explanation for my relationship with food. Sitting in a restaurant, I feel like I must apologize to the waiter for my order. If I'm on a diet, the waiter will know. If I'm about to flip out on a richly caloric jamboree, I want the waiter to forgive me. How nuts is this? Good God, the waiter is a stranger.

There are people much heavier and sicker than me who do not publicize their food obsessions. They are discreet, possibly secretive or embarrassed. They keep the insanity to themselves. With me, it's forever a subject on my lips. I think I want to change that. I know I need to.

## August 29th

I am a full eight weeks into the Weight Watchers point system. Theoretically, I can eat whatever kinds of food I want. There are no restrictions. All I have to do is make honest calculations and good choices. Instead of strict guidelines like restricting flour and sugar, today the responsibility for my gastronomic ingestion is solely mine.

According to the deal, I must construct my day around twenty-six points. A piece of fruit is good for between half a point and a point. (You do get three free fruits a day.) Two slices of diet bread equal a point. Vegetables, raw or cooked, are free and clear, devoid of points. Hurray!

For the last eight weeks, I have put together a varied and rich set of meals. I have even gone out to lots of restaurants and have enjoyed spontaneous snacks. Somehow, it doesn't feel like I'm dieting.

Here's the thing: I am definitely a member of the oral club. I still derive enormous pleasure from the act of chewing and swallowing. I cannot get away from this. I am not sure I have to get away from this. Eating is a pleasure and shouldn't be turned into a perverse pathology.

Nobody ever said that in order to be spiritually refined, you must never draw pleasure from anything in life. No one ever defined sanity as the absence of joy and delight. I am looking out my window at gorgeous roses. Seeing gorgeous roses outside my window thrills me. Touching their velvety petals has always knocked me out. The smell of a fragrant rose is one of life's greatest pleasures. Should I deny myself this?

I suppose when my body is finally a physical

representation of sound mental health, I won't feel so ashamed of deriving pleasure from the taste of Skippy chunky peanut butter.

Still, as shitty as this may sound, I thank God every day that this is as sick as I let it get. I'm glad I've never turned to liquor, sex, gambling or Valium. I don't know how I could have lived with myself, seeking comfort from the treacherous things out there. I was spared. Because I understand compulsion so well, I know that it is only by the grace of God that I have not ventured into the mire of addiction. This babyish need to overeat is as far as I am willing to go.

It served me through the hard times of my childhood, when my psychic pain was unendurable. It served me through my adolescence, when my identity was in such a precarious state. Today, I choose to examine myself more honestly and make sane choices.

I had a glass of white wine the other day at sunset on the beach. I genuinely thought it might be a great way to chill out at the end of a long, hard week. I secretly harbored the notion that I might allow this to become a once-a-week journey to the wild side. Well, guess what? A few minutes into the wine, which I drank on a fairly empty stomach, I felt a pleasant, disorienting buzz. After that, forget it. In vino veritas, right? I opened such a horrible big mouth to my dear friend Eva. I told her she was trashing her gifts as a human being, that she was just cruising in life, a time waster. I gave her such a downpour of uncalled for, unloving "truth." She didn't deserve it, poor thing. She knew it was the wine talking, for the most part, and didn't bother to defend herself.

So much for white wine; I swore it off the same night.

I know this is the right path to be on. In my heart, there is no doubt that it is only through the systematic elimination of my crutches that I can truly begin to walk again on my own two feet.

## September 3rd

Well, I got a nasty shock last night at Weight Watchers. Having been basically a good girl for the week, I was positive I had lost close to four or five pounds. Imagine my surprise when the Weight Watchers group leader weighed me and she wasn't smiling. I had gained a pound back, bringing my total weight loss since June to ten.

In the real world, nobody should care about gaining a pound… unless they've been dieting like a son of a gun for two weeks running.

I was crestfallen. I'm easy to read and the whole room knew I was heartbroken. Here I was trying so hard to diet, to match my body with my mind and spirit, and all I had was a ridiculous extra pound of fat.

I expected fairness; I expected to be rewarded for my efforts. I can't figure out what held me back. Was I wrong to expect that a satisfying result would come from my struggles?

There is a Hebrew expression: "Do not open your mouth to the devil." When you brag about success, it's seen as an invitation to the Evil Eye. Is the assumption here that you cannot acknowledge how well you are doing? Am I to believe that the universe is just lying in wait, planning a strategy to humble me?

It is entirely perverse that when I start to run down the list of all my incredible accomplishments, all the foods I've eliminated, all the seriousness with which I chronicle every food I eat—my pride invites disaster. It isn't just a matter of the weight I lose, or don't lose; the stumbling blocks that pop up can be mental, too. Even my victories can remind me of all the challenges I have yet to overcome. Often, self-satisfaction gives way to a growing sense of inadequacy.

Take the case of my long abstinence from bulimia coming up in conversation. I am, of course, very proud of such a record. Yet it is hardly my own doing, but rather an act of God; I'll be the first to admit it. My own self-control continues to let me down every time I overeat, even if I *have* given up purging. As I tell the story of my miracle, I subconsciously acknowledge the fact that I haven't achieved complete mastery over my food addiction.

I *must* learn to change this kind of thinking if I don't want to find myself scratching around for food like a hen in the barnyard. I prefer to keep on with my program and cross my fingers.

## *September 8th*

As I was coming up the steps to my office just now, I realized that my super-conscious monitoring of my moods could be likened to that of a musician or an athlete checking his performance. You know when you are on target and you know when you are off. It is not difficult at all to learn how to sensitize yourself to all the nuances of your performance ability.

I don't call the doctor if I am a touch off, mind you.

But I sure as hell do everything in my power to raise my enthusiasm meter. Because I am not your usual kind of addict, I guess I always tempered the situation by stuffing myself. Today I am making Herculean efforts to feel what I feel, truly experience what I am going through and not louse up the picture by overeating.

Case in point: An email was awaiting me at my office computer. It was from a dear friend who felt compelled to add me to his list in a chain letter. He had forwarded a personality test based on Tibetan principles, along with blessings from the Dalai Lama.

I fell into the trap, took the dumb test and even made a wish, as the letter ordered. The test was OK but I can't imagine how much validity it has. It was a self-indulgent exploration that told me what I already knew: I am smart, loving and adorable. I guess the part that made me nuts was the promise that if I made a wish, it would come true. Says who?

I deplore these idiotic intrusions, promising me that what I've always wished for will come true–just as long as I toss this hot potato to at least fifteen people.

When I scrolled down to the part about earning spiritual wealth based on the number of superstitious people I succeeded in choking with this letter, I put an end to the whole thing and deleted it. I despise people preying on insecurity. It is a loathsome trick to scare people into some kind of submission. Who dares claim they know the laws of the universe? What kind of nerve is it to send this ostensibly benign letter in hopes that you will pass it on and scare some more people?

How does all this relate to my addiction? It's simple.

I felt so aggravated by this whole episode, I wanted to eat cookies. This thinking is the habit of a lifetime. I am constitutionally capable of declining to eat, of rising above the urge. But do not for one minute think it doesn't crop up every time I feel something unpleasant.

I am becoming more and more acutely aware of which situations and thoughts make me run to food. I've even created a cute little way of describing the intensity of my emotions, my own personal Richter scale. Extremely bad news or challenges beyond my grasp rate hefty portions of my favorite nonsense. Even when I'm in control of these urges, I still assess how much food would be needed to dull the pain I am feeling.

This is a manifestation of a certain kind of crazy thinking—the kind it was hard for me to admit, at first, was crazy at all. Who was I kidding? Even while dieting successfully, enjoying periods of relatively normal weight, I've always continued to lust after certain very rich and forbidden foods. I scheme about meals, daydreaming about serious dips into the larder.

Food is always catching up with me; it has always ruled me. I do not, in any measure, have a casual relationship with food. Quite the opposite.

In spite of my obvious accomplishments and an extremely high-functioning existence, there is no logic or sanity in the way I have, historically, managed my relationship with food. On this subject, I have been a moron, inconsistent and ridiculous.

When I joined OA, I hated admitting powerlessness. It went against my fundamental belief that I was the predominant creative force in my life. I was initially afraid that if

I admitted powerlessness, I would not be shaping my own destiny. If I made right choices, I was the commander, right?

But though I was reluctant to admit I was powerless over food, I had to at least admit that I was powerless over food thoughts.

Step Two is when you come to believe that a power greater than yourself can restore you to sanity. I know I didn't take too well to this accusation–that I was insane. In my mind, except for the food madness, I was more sane and wise and funny and loving than anyone. It took me a long time to admit that I was an honest to goodness food addict, and therefore, a sane person living in an insane way. This may sound like a semantic game, but there is an unmistakable element of insanity inside every addict, irrespective of how high-functioning he or she is.

Let's not forget Bill Clinton's temporary fall from grace. He obviously was unable to tame his irresistible urges; they made him take ridiculous risks. He was not labeled insane, nor dismissed as a lunatic. He was a sane person acting in an insane manner. Victimized by his cravings, he did what any addict would do.

Bill's thing was ladies. George W. Bush had a hankering for booze and cocaine. Countless other people in high places gamble their souls away. Irrespective of how and what, we're all in the same boat. I am the president of cookies and peanut butter; they were the presidents of the United States.

## *September 12th*

I didn't have much energy today for my exercise practice. My coach, my younger son, was dismayed when I told him how low my average pulse was. He said that I had wasted forty minutes on the ride. When I was doing my stretches after this poor excuse for physical fitness, I glanced down at my legs. They looked unsightly.

That's an interesting expression–unsightly. Does it mean that the spectacle is so horrendous that it would better if no one lay eyes on this ghastly scene?

I have unsightly legs? I have legs that should not be on public display? How do you think that feels? When is this ever going to be right?

Which will happen first? Will I lose the weight and fall in love with my legs, or will I accept them as they are, love them anyway, and watch them as they get more shapely and sightly?

I got into bed early at the end of the day, feeling crappy. I'd had a long day and was in a crappy mood. It was hot and muggy outside and I had absolutely no intention of accompanying my husband to a concert at the Music Academy. Michael kept begging me and I kept begging off. I made ridiculous excuses just to ensure that I would have the house to myself, the stage set for a little food festival. It was a private party. Gatecrashers–beware!

I shooed him out and started down the highway between the bed and the fridge. At least I had the wherewithal to stick to fruit salad with salted almonds and pistachios, stopping there even though it hadn't quite done the trick. And then I began to consider the notion of "doing the trick for me."

You see, I was in a stinky mood. I was also ashamed of the fact that I had ripped my husband off by not going with him to the concert. He felt obligated to go and does not give himself excuses for things like bad humidity. I often let the lazy part of my nature take over and immobilize me. Naturally, I felt guilty. Naturally, that was hard to bear. Naturally, I turned to food to ease me out of these painful emotions. "To do the trick" for me was to get rid of feeling like a failure to both myself and my husband.

What exactly would do the trick could never be ingested. My problem was emotional; my guilt and shame would not be assuaged by solutions that did nothing to address them. How could they be?

As a little girl, my thumb-sucking, my nail-biting, and, of course, my food seemed to numb me out and lower my tension. They gave me hours of relief and pleasure. It never occurred to me that I was avoiding something or replacing something. I didn't understand that my behavior was metaphorical. All I knew was that I had these habits. I couldn't stop them. I loved them and had no desire to ease them out of my repertoire. They were *me*. They were how I saw myself.

Now my view of myself is changing. I am sophisticated enough to have a theory about my behavior. Obviously, I have far more psychological savvy. I am no longer a loser; I do not have to be stuck with these embarrassing, childish behaviors.

## *September 26th*

I did a sneak-peek at the scale: three months of effort have yielded a loss of fourteen pounds.

I rarely do this anymore. I do not spend my days yanking the scale out from under the bathroom sink and noting every ounce of progress. I am training myself to delay my gratification. I am weighed once weekly at Weight Watchers and the exact amount I lose comes as a surprise. It is never as much as I wish for. I know I am being unrealistic, I know that slow and steady is the way to go, but I am dealing with numbers I haven't seen for almost forty years here.

These new, extra twenty-five pounds that have crept up on me are an abomination. Hell, I have been at this for three months. Three months of diet and exercise? In the old days, I would have been a showstopper by now. I would have been sitting pretty and taking bows. Very well-deserved bows. I like it when people notice; I bask in the accomplishment of such a serious feat.

This is more complicated than vanity. In many ways, I am significantly less preoccupied than others with personal appearance. I wear the barest minimum of eye make-up and put myself together casually. I spend almost no time in front of the mirror; I've never seen the value of staring myself down, looking for wrinkles and the like.

So why in hell, if this is such a spiritual journey, am I wasting my time wondering what I will look like thirty or fifty pounds thinner? I always like to say that nothing will change, exactly. I will be in superior physical shape, giving my heart and lungs a well-deserved vacation. Indubitably, people who know me will be amazed and thrilled. I will feel a sense of accomplishment and peace will descend on the planet.

See, that's the problem. Am I losing weight for world peace? Am I doing this so there will never be famine or disease on the face of the earth? I wish. I wish I could delude myself into believing this is a gesture I am making for humanity, instead of a project designed to make things a little easier for ME ME ME.

Lord, forgive me my small vanity and egocentrism. I deserve to know what life will be like when the fatsuit is tossed in the flames and I rise from the smoke much more angelic than when I started.

## October 9th

I cannot fail to address the issue I call My Clothing. On the rare occasions I dress up, I tend toward a more costume-ish look. My mother used to call my clothing "that getup." I recall an incident that occurred at the opera during my New York years, when I was already maintaining a good figure. After she inquired how much my latest secondhand dress cost me, she handed over four crisp ten-dollar bills and asked me never to wear it again in her presence: "It does nothing for you, darling."

I recently came across an old picture of myself in that dress and I could not get over how snappy I looked. I was stunning.

I have a handsome suit that I wore almost twenty years ago while hosting a reception for my girlfriend Tovah, the Broadway star. I looked so good in it that she was forced to say to me in all sincerity: "Good God, Elle, you're thinner than I am." That compliment still rings in my ears. That suit is still in my closet. I am close to fifty pounds away from getting into it, but I can't bring myself to chuck it out. It is grossly out of style, maybe even faded, but that pantsuit is a symbol of success and sanity. If I can ever fit into it again, it will be an achievement of immense proportions.

It will not just be about losing weight this time. Of course not. It will be about the successful investigation and eradication of my distorted ego, duplicity, guilt, fear, anger and all the other pesky, well-hidden sides that I have chosen to bring into the light.

Almost a decade ago, I was in New York, staying at the guesthouse of a good friend, Erica, a gal well past seventy who has since passed away. I absolutely adored her. She was powerful, astute and said what was on her mind.

I needed an outfit to wear to my husband's art opening. I was heavier than I had been the last time I saw Erica and her sister Lucy, but I didn't realize just how much heavier.

Erica and Lucy were very elegant and well-groomed. They knew how and where to shop. I am mighty weak in that department. I have lived in the Middle East for decades and let go of my shopping muscles a long time ago. I stink as a shopper. So when I announced that I was a size fourteen, Lucy and Erica said, in the most perfectly synchronized chant: "No, Ellie, you are not."

What a hoot. Those two weren't fooled by my self-deception. I must have looked like a cool eighteen.

I marched myself into the large-size department at Saks, overpaying for a dress I didn't end up wearing. I settled instead for rather basic black trousers and a marvelous colored African-print tunic. I felt safer in that getup than in the dress, which bared more of my calves than I was willing to flaunt.

If you want to torture me to death, take me shopping and make me stand in the little cubicle under the traditionally unflattering fluorescent lights. Force me to look at myself as I put on and take off the items being considered for purchase. Always, to my most painful consternation, there will be that moment when I am caught in my bra and panties and the bulges and unsightly cellulite stare back at me. I feel like the world's ugliest excuse for a middle-aged woman. I want to die right there and then in the booth.

Mirrors are decidedly not my best friends. They mar my experience even in restaurants. Just when I'm feeling good about myself, a quick trip to the ladies' room can bring me right back down. As I zip up my pants, I see the same thing that drove my mother nuts till the day she died: a recently acquired and very unwelcome body part that has taken up residence between the top of my pants and my bra. Maybe this is what they call a midriff bulge?

We middle-aged gals fall into thinking that Lycra in our shirts holds us in and makes us look thinner. This is a grievous mistake. It only accentuates the disfigurement.

As skinny as my mother was, she too had this physical accusation of aging on her, which she could not bear. I highly doubt that mine will go away any time soon. What can I say? I'll have to live with it, or undergo some nip and tuck if it becomes too freaky on the new, slimmed-down version of Ellie. I'll have to cross that bridge when I come to it.

## *October 13th*

Speaking of mirrors. On my way to the shower after a vigorous bike ride, I caught a glimpse of myself in the bathroom. I was disappointed. Despite my daily mantra–"Patience,

Ellie"—I somehow expected that after four months of reasonably serious endeavor, I should look better. But what I saw was the result of years of bad food management and middle age.

I was alone, supposedly getting ready for a rendezvous with friends. I got on my bed and began to weep. I wept with frustration, disappointment and sadness. I wept with anger and shame. I called my friends, sobbing. I told them I might not be coming.

When I hung up with them, it suddenly dawned on me that my naked body might look flabby and fleshy but, hello, I am taking real steps to straighten things out. I am eating well, I am exercising; short of major surgery there is nothing else I *could* be doing to improve things. Even without the overnight change I crave, I know that I am doing well.

Enough. I called the girls and told them I would meet them in an hour. I did not need to perpetuate my misery by wallowing in it. I was able to see things from a clearer perspective. I got the point and the feedback that the mirror offers. It was enough to fall apart for a few cathartic minutes and move on.

On the ride to Tel Aviv, the following occurred to me: If a person wants to be a doctor, a huge time factor is at play until the dream is actualized. Amassing an education and putting it into practice takes time. Maybe if I think of this journey as an education, beginner to advanced training, I won't feel so resentful about time. After all, I don't want to be an orderly; I want to be the doctor.

I love that. This thought is enormously encouraging. It pleases me to be reassured by mature, rational thought and not by thumb-sucking or Mars bars. My expectations have to be more realistic. Over time, I will learn better coping mechanisms. Over time, with proper eating and exercise, the small movements of the scale will add up! And so will the small changes in my head.

## October 29th

Boy, oh boy, have I been waiting to write. We just came back from a spectacular visit to the States. We spent the first few days with my brother Lewis at his place in New York. He hosted us like royalty; our heartfelt, nostalgic, funny conversations lasted for hours. We have an unusual rapport. We bounce off of each other's humor. As different as we are stylistically, we *get* each other and treasure our shared history.

It's the first time in almost fifty years that my brother is unattached. As I say those words, I feel sad and glad, both at once. I think it is a good thing that my brother is separated from his wife; I don't believe their relationship was good for him anymore. Of course, I'm sad that he is alone. If anyone deserves to be in a loving relationship, it's my beautiful brother Lewis.

I have every reason to believe there is a woman out there who will be right for him and that he will have his opportunity to celebrate his life with a human being who is truly appropriate. It will be a welcome change and a reason to rejoice.

I must say, though, that my brother is faring beautifully as a single man. Since the separation, he has traveled extensively and managed to enjoy his life. I'm looking forward to our next reunion; we're talking about a late April caper in Holland. He's heard about our annual visit to the flower show and wants to join.

Now that I'm home, I'm enjoying getting back to my usual routine. I had a fine night's sleep, beating the jetlag, and woke up very cheerful and snuggly.

There will always be challenges and setbacks, but if you are lucky there will also be lovely times when you are flowing smoothly with life and things feel terrific. Why not? Whenever this happens, I am not too stingy to thank the universe for my good fortune. A good moment, for no apparent reason, is a gift from above.

## *November 2nd*

I am not your typical control freak. Most people never know how much I revel in order and harmony. But I need to feel that things are in hand. I need to feel safe in the world of cause-and-effect relationships. When things go smoothly, with little delightful surprises, I celebrate. I am relaxed and optimistic; this is my Eden, my version of perfection.

Most of the time I embrace life on its terms, tenderly accepting ironies, mishaps and setbacks. When I am in my right mind, relaxed and happy, I field any blows in good humor and wisdom. I am patient.

But I have been known to lose the battle with my best self. At such times, I react to life and its challenges in a most unimpressive manner. When my warrior skills weaken, I can fall prey to the food demons. Those little rascals–those hungry stinkers–stand around with their mouths open, begging. They live by the slogan "More is never enough." When they rear their ugly heads and flex their muscles, it's hard to ignore them. Good sense tells me to keep them at arm's length, to pretend they don't exist. But they are insistent. They wait for the moment when I trip and fall into the abyss. It always sends them shrieking. Their wails are deafening. The only way I can shut them up is by shoveling food down my gullet.

This is the only explanation I can offer for my behavior yesterday.

This is how the day began: While I was meditating, I realized that my heart was pounding. My blood pressure generally hovers at ninety over sixty, so I knew immediately that something was very wrong. I deduced that the conventional medication I was taking was duking it out with the Chinese herbs that Hila, my beloved acupuncturist, had given me. I made a hasty call to announce to Hila that the herbs seemed to have boomeranged on me and she told me to stop taking them.

After that, everything I tried to accomplish went awry. My communication with people was muddled and unpleasant. I even sensed a lack of coordination, as if something was off in my brain. I kept dropping things. I had to do an errand in my car and something told me disaster was on the horizon. Sure enough, I managed to bump into a telephone pole.

This fiasco was the last straw. I drove home and decided to cancel the entire rest of the day. I phoned some people, exaggerating slightly about the extent of the accident, using this as a way to weasel out of my obligations.

Having done that, I had a heady feeling of power. I

could cancel my day and get away with it. I am, by nature, a very responsible person, a pathological people-pleaser who pales at the idea of disappointing anybody. But with the car mishap in my pocket, I milked the situation dry. Maybe it was an act of self-protection, putting a halt to any further catastrophe.

All alone in my house, I kicked off my shoes and set the stage for a party.

Now, don't forget: I'm allowed twenty-six Weight Watchers points a day. What I am describing is the outrageous consumption of fifteen points in thirty minutes. It was like I was trying to break a record. I consumed bread and butter, ice cream, and a banana mashed into a bowl of rice. I managed to limit myself to *diet* ice cream bars, at least, and the bread was thin-sliced and whole wheat.

As I finished my last forkful, I realized that the sated food demons had had their fill and were once again silenced.

I took to my bed, an uncustomary act, and dove into an amazing book about the Holocaust. Two pages into 1943 in Poland and I was feeling drowsy. Just for the record, I do not usually nap. I am constitutionally incapable of shutting my head off during the day. I have always looked in awe at people who lose consciousness and slip into afternoon sleep.

The food, wolfed down in such a short span of time, must have left me in a state of inebriation that my brain could not tolerate. Two hours later, covered in drool, I woke up dazed and grateful for the escape. Frankly, I was dumbfounded. I never have things like that happen to me.

The next morning, I still felt lousy and proceeded to tell my nearest and dearest that I'd been poisoned by the

Chinese herbs. It was going to take some time till I could trust my brain again. It was frustrating that I had no choice but to wait it out.

By the grace of God, my dear friend Udel called. Instead of pampering me and encouraging me to wallow in self-pity, she gave me a pep talk that would befit a coach in the NBA. She has a booming voice and gets worked up when I have crossed certain lines of mental health.

All I did was tell her I'd had a bad morning. Udel screamed from her cell phone about how I am like one of the junkies she and I both treat. We have a full roster of clients who range from heroin and cocaine addictions to serious, scary bulimia. According to her, I have a serious addiction to feeling good. The minute something is slightly off, I catastrophize. She begged me to understand that everybody on the planet has bad days, can wake up on the wrong side of the bed, and so forth.

"Get over yourself, Ellie. Stop looking for the answer somewhere else! Stop running to another healer, herbalist or clairvoyant. I am sick of this—when are you going to wake up?" She was screaming at the top of her lungs in the thickest New Jersey accent I have ever heard.

I had to strap myself in restraints to keep a civil tongue in my mouth. I adore her and a lot of what she says makes sense, especially the parts that remind me to straighten up and act my age. The thing of it is that I am such an emotional idiot sometimes. Instead of using my gifts to create shifts in my mood, I fall apart and freak out.

I do have a hard time feeling bad. I don't like apprehension. It humiliates me. I don't want anything to do with resentment; it makes me feel like the rest of the world when I prefer to see myself as evolved. And sadness—the thick, gooey depression that grabs you by the throat, descending on you and making everything unattainable and pointless—who the hell wants that?

I thank my lucky stars that my freak-outs usually pass in a short span of time. Being such a child, however, I feel I must give a progress report to all of my near and dear as events occur. If only I could just let bad moments pass without all the fanfare. It's possible for me to change, I know it now. Just like everything else I've ever worked on and succeeded with, it is just a matter of sincere dedication to the task.

That little weasel Udel just called me back to check up on me. I love her for it.

"Are you feeling better now, big baby?"

"As a matter of fact I am, doll. I owe you a lot for shaking me up this morning. Believe it or not, I am changing. The progression in my life toward maturity is unmistakable. Thanks to your 'Everyone on the planet has bad days' speech, I now realize that as much as I hate the idea, I am part of that *everyone.* Thank you for caring so deeply."

## *November 3rd*

I am in the car, edging toward the group, our leader, Ziv Tal, and the scale that never lies. Ziv is a real character. She has a stage-self as outrageous as a diva. Her wardrobe is endless. Just being in her presence is enough to motivate a room of one hundred fat souls to put down the silly gobbling and end the insanity once and for all. I absolutely adore her and normally look forward to hearing her bark at us until she is hoarse.

As I walk in, there are new faces, at least five or six, and almost none of the old crowd. I wonder if this isn't a sign. I take my seat in room, which is only nominally full, and wait for my turn at the scale.

Ziv calls me up for my weigh-in. I whisper: "Never mind. It's not important."

Her face tells me: "Get over yourself, Ellie, and step on the scale."

I comply. After all, she's the group leader and she knows this stuff inside-out. Here I need to take a leap of faith.

I start with my usual *schtick* of one leg only on the scale. She says: "Let's go, Ellie. Stand up straight. Two feet, please. I promise not to tell you what you weigh." She is referring to the little contract we've established: she tells me how much I've lost or gained, but she never reveals my actual weight. For crying out loud, why do I still remain such a jerk about this?

Anyway, she says: "Look, it's not that bad. You lost a hundred grams. I want to strategize an eating plan with you; try it for a few weeks. Give up your attachment to spontaneity. Do what you're told. Let it work and the rest will be history."

The meeting is about to begin and I take my seat. Ziv looks directly at me when she asks if anyone in the room wants to share some of his or her successes or failures over the last week.

I speak up. Because most of the crowd are newcomers, they seem fairly reluctant to give me advice.

At the meeting's end, a group forms around Ziv. They

are jabbering away in Hebrew and I feel like an outsider. Decades of living in Israel have done nothing to make me feel I truly belong here. The second I start to speak, people either imitate my pronunciation or switch to English to show off their bilingual skills, assuming all the while that because of my accent I must either be fresh off the boat or linguistically stunted, so they'd better stick to my native tongue.

So here I am, on the fringes of this enthusiastic crowd of Israeli Weight Watchers. I guess I am looking pretty beat, especially after delivering my story of personal failure. I wait patiently, hoping for a minute of Ziv's time. Before my turn comes, a lady on my right says to me in English with a thick Israeli accent, "Stop."

I say to her, "What did you say?"

She says it again: "Stop." It sounds like *stawp*. She really draws out the middle of this one-syllable word.

I think I might faint. So many aspects of this touch me. First of all, it is bold. One word delivered spontaneously in English says so much. This is no speech, no long list of admonitions, no advice-giving. She is not expressing any desire to share words of wisdom or her own personal success story. She just opened her mouth and out came a miracle.

I give her a kiss.

All the soul-searching, all the nit-picking, won't help me much if I don't stop the compulsive overeating. *Stop* is such an extraordinary concept. It requires nothing from me. It's the *not* doing. It's the *no* effort. Well, there is an inherent effort I will have to make in the beginning. That effort is to remember to stop, even when I feel like going along my merry way, gobbling everything in sight.

As I leave, Ziv leans over and says to me, using an expression I've never heard before: "Ellie, I'm counting on you to bring me some weight loss next week. Can you do that?"

Nobody has ever asked that of me before.

I get the feeling that Ziv wants me to give over the pain attached to my padding. In her complete generosity, it feels like she is saying, "Give it to me, Ellie. I will take care of it and make sure you never need it again." There is something in her face, a look in her eyes that says: "There is no doubt in my mind that you are entirely capable of doing this. I sincerely wish, with all my heart, Ellie dear, that whatever force is still ruling you, forcing you to plunge again and again into the food, will be conquered."

I start playing with the idea that I am lucky enough to know a turning point when I see one.

Oh, how I pray this is true. What spiritual advancement, to actually be present when something gigantic is happening to you. I feel so touched and hope this feeling never leaves me.

## November 4th

Here I am, just into the fifth month of this immense challenge.

I have lost the first twenty pounds! This is real and indisputable. Unfortunately, it is not glaringly visible. I remain a chubette rather than a tall, handsome woman or a slim one. A little voice inside snottily tells me: "What's the big victory? You never should have been so neurotic to begin with. You shouldn't have gotten fat in the first place.

Stephanie always used to remind me that the Dalai Lama wears glasses. "Elle, do you think he beats himself up daily because he needs to wear spectacles so he can see? Trust me, he doesn't. He's obviously more mature than you are."

So I'm still betting on my success. Despite some slips, my overall direction is satisfying. Credit where credit's due! I can proudly say that I have been on my exercise bike over a hundred times. I have ridden approximately 1,200 miles. I have sweated buckets and I have heard Gloria Estefan so much, she is coming out of my ears. I am certain the next twenty pounds will make a huge difference and I will feel my progress more tangibly.

I have a lot of work yet to do on myself if I am to truly get to the finish line by next summer. My being is already undergoing revision and renewal. But I am not so foolish as to imagine that I will ever reach the ultimate refinement of my character. I will always be a work in progress.

One of the things I love about the Twelve Steps is Step Ten, which refers to the continuity of the process, the ongoing nature of spiritual evolution: *Continued to take personal inventory, and when we were wrong, promptly admitted it.* You don't do Step Four–*Made a searching and fearless moral inventory*–once and for all. You need to keep a watchful eye on yourself, staying alert and abreast of every little nuance and twist in your interactions.

These guidelines are an impeccable bible for living well. When honored, they can take you to spiritual and emotional heights you could never otherwise envision.

## November 6th

I have been going to Pilates for the last five years. In these past few months, I have been taking my classes very seriously, devoting myself to progress. Yet even though I've lost twenty pounds, there are some activities that are still extremely uncomfortable because of my girth. When I lie on my back and hold my legs up in the air, something obnoxious occurs: my belly, midriff and bosom converge in a mass of blubber that presses against my throat as I hold my legs up in the air. There is less of me than there was before, I'll give you that. But, although I am in much better shape than I was, I feel blue. I am aggravated by this blubber. I can't believe that I have done this to myself.

One day at a time.

One day at a time is one of the powerful messages in Twelve-Step recovery programs. I just need to live well and be well one day at a time. I don't need to get involved today in the mathematics of months down the road, minus a few of my body's spare tires. No, that won't get me anywhere. That is guaranteed to lock me into a mindset totally oriented to a future that may or may not come to fruition. I need to find joy and serenity today, accepting myself just where I am for now.

## November 11th

Everything I hold sacred tells me that mood rules. When I'm in a good mood, I am absolutely capable and ready for my life. I deal with challenges and take care of business with a smile. Little things excite me and I am in a constant state of very OK. I am on the higher side of happy. It takes very little to thrill me. That's why I know how hellish and gruesome it is when my mood is compromised.

I think I want to mention this: Quite a few years ago, menopause hit me like a bomb, complete with vicious mood swings as well as ceaseless hot flashes that roused me from my slumber up to ten times a night. Anyone who tries to glorify menopause is either a man or a liar. It is horribly unfunny. One could possibly find the hot flashes and desperate fanning off comical at first, but after you have observed several of these episodes in an hour, the heart-wrenching desperation they cause should inspire only sympathy in the public.

It was very hard to stay emotionally afloat with all this.

Then, in the space of a year and ten days, I lost both my parents. That blow was devastating. It took an effort to smile and be enthusiastic. Melancholy grayed my days. While I could function and live productively, something vital was missing. The loneliness of being twice orphaned in such a short time, the constant battle with my mood and hot flashes, the desperation to find relief–all of this wore me out. I struggled to find my *joie de vivre*. I became someone argumentative and cranky, an alien to myself. I felt overwhelmed. It was nightmarish.

The only recourse I had was to find some system, some treatment that would straighten out this horrible state. After nothing in the world of alternative medicine could help me–and I tried *everything*–I turned to conventional medications in order to tame the menopausal monster.

This embarrassed me terribly. I felt like a charlatan. The queen of natural medicine, the most seasoned meditator on the block, couldn't handle hot flashes, mood swings and mourning. *She* had to take medicine to cope.

This year, I have been learning to accept that sometimes my moods will be hard to escape. But today my husband, despite my initial reluctance, succeeded in lifting up my melancholy. When I awoke feeling blue this morning, his solution was to march me up a nearby mountain. In the beginning, he was practically dragging my dead weight. To any witnesses, the two of us must have looked like a cartoon of a man trying to *schlep* a cranky mule.

On the walk down the mountain, it suddenly hit me—the panorama and all that quiet; how lovely. I opened my heart to the mood enhancement that nature inevitably renders. I started to feel better, against my will.

I thank God that today, I'm not in the place I was during the tsunami that was my menopause.

## *November 12th*

I am in search of a mind/body practitioner. I think that I need to have some external input; I have been doing this *on my own* for too long. I got the name of a deep-tissue masseuse ten minutes from my house and gave her a call. I was open to the experience, although not entirely sure at first that this type of massage would provide the relaxation plus heightened body awareness that I need.

When I got to the clinic, which was in a garage, I was immediately struck by the sweetness of Isella. The cave-like setting was decorated with candles, colored fabrics and a coziness that promised a relaxing experience.

The massage was like nothing I had ever done before.

In fact, I would hardly call it a massage. I was a little puzzled at the instruction to remain fully clothed; how would she be able to reach my tissues in a deep manner, as suggested by the very title of her technique?

Isella asked permission before placing her hands on me. This high degree of respect shown to me just added to my appreciation of this woman. As she moved from geography to geography on my physical self, I felt something opening in my spirit.

She realized that I was a little surprised by the technique she was offering, and, bless her soul, she did nothing to make me feel foolish and unschooled. I want to receive all the tricks up her sleeve. I will be seeing her again next week.

## *November 16th*

Slowly and surely, my hard work is starting to be reflected in my clothes. I am wearing pants I could not possibly have fit into in June. A poor and reluctant shopper, I bought these pale lavender seersucker trousers for twenty-nine dollars, even though they were too small. The color and material made me pass out with joy. Never mind the fact that they didn't fit. I knew my closet would never be lonely and blue with these pants on a hanger.

I dare to dream that when the time comes to take out my summer clothes again, they will be too ridiculously large to consider. Some big, lucky girl will be the recipient of the items that won't fit me anymore.

I cannot deny that I am feeling very powerful. Things are falling into place today and I am infused with good, working optimism. I am getting carried away and imagining giving endless workshops as a slim, recovered me, the living example, the graceful embodiment of liberation. No longer a slave to whatever excessive eating was doing for me, I am beginning to enjoy my body again.

"With the help of the good Lord," one of my mother's favorite phrases, I will achieve my goal and light the way for others. As I was dressing this morning, I dreamed up a new program called "Enough of the Nonsense!" It would be my honor to help people get over their nonsense in a fun way. I don't want to be responsible for every detail of their lives, but I want to rouse people from psychic slumber and then move on to the next group of strugglers. I prefer to see myself as a teacher rather than a therapist.

## November 21st

Last night, I hosted an elegant champagne concert event. I was in charge of the arrangements and took care to hire a very sophisticated catering service.

I debated all day as to whether or not I was going to be completely unglued by the cuisine. On the one hand, I told myself, "Relax, kid, what are you making such a big stink about one night for?" The attorney for the defense of my sanity said: "Why start? Even if you stay within your points, think how triumphant you will feel after the party, knowing you were not compelled to indulge in all that sugar and flour. Enjoy the evening with a glass of diet Sprite in your hand and keep circulating. You'll be better off without champagne bubbles jamming up your consciousness. Remember what happened with the white wine a few months ago?"

I was the first to have a glass of champagne. I had it on an empty stomach, the stomach I obviously readied for the evening's ingestion. I was tipsy after a few sips. I wasn't particularly thinking. Just to be a big shot, just to play the consummate hostess, I sipped that champagne and flitted around the room like a fairy princess. I was gracious and charming.

By the evening's end, I'd had two glasses of champagne to damage my judgment. The food was quite impressive and I tasted everything. I was particularly wowed by the pumpkin soup served in espresso cups.

When dessert was dished out, I had one forkful of each kind of cake. One was a lemony tart with meringue; it was a delightful play between sweet and sour. One was an obscenity featuring three different kinds of chocolate. I never think desserts are too rich, but this was bordering on the insane. The third cake was the closest to reasonable of all of them. It was made with a whole wheat crust and filled with apples and pears, laced with hints of vanilla, lemon zest and cinnamon.

I'm still not sure which way I want to go when it comes to forkfuls of cake. While it is hardly much of an incident calorically, there's a sneaky part to it that I don't relish. It still feels like I'm cheating.

In my home meeting of OA, almost all of the members keep a very rigid abstinence, which is vaguer and more subjective than in other Twelve-Step programs. For example, if you are in Alcoholics Anonymous, sobriety is defined as not drinking alcoholic beverages. It's not abstract. In

Gamblers Anonymous, abstinence is defined by the elimination of betting. With food, a must in all of our lives, abstinence necessitates the elimination of compulsive *over*eating. Since this is so tricky to envision, and since we all must have daily interactions with food, many people in the program create guidelines with their sponsors of essential *do*s and *don't*s.

For many people in the program, abstinence means complete liberation from sugar and white flour. For others, it is the elimination of carbohydrates except for a fruit or two a day. The food plan one establishes with the sponsor might well be based on some prior discussion with a nutritionist. The most extreme forms of abstinence I've heard about involve the commitment to three meals a day, weighed and measured, with nothing in between, no snacks. Many people following plans of this nature don't even chew sugarless gum or drink Diet Cola. Lord, have mercy.

There are members who consider themselves deviant if they eat in between meals. They consider themselves "slipped" if they eat a carrot as a snack. I do not want to live that way. I want to distance myself from that thinking. My hope in these last five months has been to develop a comfortable relationship with my plate and not a fear of foods. There are no bad foods. It's not about the food!

Ellie's sanity vis-à-vis food is: "Eat and enjoy; treat yourself as a blessed entity." As long as I do not deify food, there should be nothing I cannot eat in measured portions. Small amounts of sugar and flour are not sinful. The occasional few bites of cake should not signify a nosedive into perdition.

I ask God daily for a reprieve from my compulsion to overeat. I want to be able to make sane choices. I want to be able to eat a bite or two of this or that, enjoy it, realize it's not that important and put it back on the plate. I don't want to overinvest in the idea that it has any power over me.

I know that this must sound like the voice of my self-deception. But I just can't see now trading obsessions and becoming hysterically afraid of food.

Sanity here is the absence of obsessive thinking and worrying about what I did and what I might do. Sanity is the healthy place where I trust that I am being watched over, safe out of harm's way. The harm that I can cause myself is born of tormented thoughts and ridiculous, inappropriate gobbling.

I must admit that champagne is a different story. This is not a moral issue or a snobbish view, scorning or pitying those who resort to the bubbly to lift their spirits and amplify the party mood. This is purely about me and my psychophysiology's reaction to the ingestion of alcohol. I have to remember that I have zero tolerance for the stuff and should keep a good distance between us.

I am lucky because my lifestyle is rather exclusively devoid of alcoholic beverages in the first place. I am almost never in contact with the liquid. This should make it easier for me to keep my mitts off of it and never play the big shot.

It's rather quaint how this subject comes up a few times a year with my husband. He is so not a drinker that he calls my occasional glasses of wine a demonstration of my playing sophisticated, grown-up lady. I love this. What a notion that I, a truly sophisticated grandma, would need a glass of champagne in my hand at a party in order to show how grown up I am.

I started smoking at thirteen. I was at an artsy-fartsy summer camp in the Berkshires. I thought cigarettes made me look older, then. Right now, I don't need to look older!

## November 24th

My birthday is in sixteen days and I've been musing about how nifty it would be to reach my birthday at the same time that I reach a thirty-pound weight-loss milestone. This is insane. I would not set such an unrealistic goal if I truly embraced the emotional complexity underlying the physical aims of this challenge. My ability to self-deceive should win me an Oscar. I fall in my own traps, biting off my foot for a snack.

In the past, the objective was to lose weight as quickly as possible. My fantasy was always to find myself a room at a very aesthetic New Age joint for a month. It would be like something in a magazine–spacious, state of the art, in pastel hues, with faint traces of rose and neroli oil in the air. The treatments, elaborate and exquisite, would have very fancy names.

I recall an out-of-body experience that I actually did have once, the "Rain Baby" event at a Santa Monica day spa. Oddly enough, the room smelled of chocolate and vanilla. I felt like I was in a bakery. I lay stark naked on a particularly wide treatment bed, anxiously awaiting the answer to why the session was given such a special name. In came a soft-voiced Amazon. Her dreadlocks almost reached her knees. She asked my name. I told her: "I'm

Ellie from Jerusalem." She replied in a breathy whisper with a slight hint of Brooklyn in her accent: "Isn't it a guy's name in Hebrew? If I'm not mistaken, it means 'my God.'"

For the next two hours, she smeared me from head to toe three times with special scented oils guaranteed to make me look and feel decades younger. Twice, as if a cloud were hovering, I was sprinkled with warm water. My entire nakedness became drenched by this heavenly shower. She dried me off with hot fluffy towels, only to begin the process all over again! She hummed as she did her job. It was very comforting, though odd.

A few times, I delicately requested some silence so I could concentrate on the magnitude of what was happening. I felt that I was coming in and out of myself. My consciousness was altered and I felt on the brink of a big Moment.

Who has ever lain naked on a table in the rain? It was an otherworldly moment in which I felt completely cared for.

Oh the joy of self-indulgent, scandalous, obscenely expensive treatments. In my fantasy, I'd have some lymph draining; I'd have them annihilate my cellulite. Who knows, maybe I'd have a little surgery thrown in. Whatever. I would enter as an under-exercised, fat representation of myself and leave a month later toned and firmed–twenty pounds thinner, dazzling. I'd come home new and evolved, a poster child of OA. My insides would of course match my outsides.

If you think for one minute that I've ever actually played this dream out, *you* must be dreaming. It's never happened. I am a working wife and mother with serious obligations. I have never afforded myself the luxury of getting away to such an extent. I am also stopped by my guilt and shame. They shout in my ear: "Why are you so unaccomplished? Why do you have to 'go somewhere' in order to get in shape?"

It's usually around this juncture that I begin to plan the next major diet.

Why am I not able to just let my birthday come and go without attaching stupid measurements of success or failure?

## *November 27th*

For two days in a row, I have been tentatively re-establishing diplomatic relations with bagels.

Ten years ago, I asked a colleague of mine at the rehab where I work to function as an additional sponsor. He was adamant about me cutting out, or "putting down," sugar and white flour. My abstinence lasted for five whole months. When I think about it, I am amazed.

At some point, I lost my grip and found myself diving into a sea of cookies. When I disclosed this to him, he suggested I write letter to God about my relationship with cookies.

I took this task seriously. I choked and wept as I wrote. It was astounding to realize how emotional I was over these doughy rounds. I had counted on them for years to get me through the tough times. I had shoved fancy and plain pastry down my throat and piled it in my body, hoping for some relief. That's all I was doing–hoping for some relief from the psychic pain. Here's the letter.

*Dear God,*

*As You know, I don't like asking for Your help. I have no problem singing Your praises—I bet You even hear my songs. I am so grateful, so aware of the gifts You shower on me.*

*But those stinkers—the cookies—have been driving me nuts. By Your grace, You lifted the bulimia years ago. Honestly, it was miraculous. You are the maker of miracles, so You put the people I need in my path, even though they can be nudniks and yentas.*

*I have been asked to ask You to help me, by Your Grace, say farewell to my best friends who have been with me forever. I have many foods I love, many tastes that have carried me through the rough times, but if I had to choose my favorite, I guess it would be the cookies. I adore cookies and can eat many of them at a sitting. I can also eat them standing up or lying down. I can eat them when they're not so tasty—I always forgive them for being less than I expect. I've eaten frozen cookies, stale cookies, other people's portions of cookies, grabbing more for me BECAUSE I NEED THEM MORE THAN ANYBODY ELSE!*

*God, I am crying as I write this. I feel like a cheater and a betrayer. They are harmless—I mistreated them and myself with my greed. They are not to blame, so why do I have to kill them off?*

*Does asking for help mean I must forever separate myself from them? What about when I NEED them? What am I going to do then? Are You going to lift me up?*

*I am asking for help and scared You will give it and then where will I be? I am scared You won't give it—and secretly hoping that You won't so that I can go on sitting in front of the TV at night with my buddies. Not every night, but special nights when nothing will work but cookies.*

*So, I am in a big mess and we both know it.*

*Help me, your faithful servant, Eleanor Doris Henkind who became Dr. Ellie Katz.*

*P.S. It was Eleanor Doris who discovered how much the cookies could help. Address her pain too!*

While I don't want to be afraid of any food, bagels, like cookies, may be too dangerous for me, at least for the moment. Should they be on my list of governments who support terrorists? Is the white flour a cruel dominatrix whipping me into submission?

I've decided that I won't touch a drop of white flour until next Friday. Then I'll see how I feel about it.

## December 2nd

I have a bone to pick with the athletes who promise that exercise brings euphoria. It's just not true for me. Bike riding is still very hard; I get sweaty and exhausted. I plod along and wonder when all that joy is going to implode in my brain.

I am now up to forty-five minutes a day and I must be pedaling faster. I have increased my ability and endurance but haven't yet found a way to adore this experience. I do it faithfully, but I just can't figure out how to milk the situation for all its endorphin potential.

I saw a documentary about a famous Israeli magician and psychic; he was skinny as a rat. He used to be bulimic and claims he no longer is. I have news for him. He turned from a vomiting bulimic into an exercise bulimic, who sits proudly astride his stationary bike for hours. Apparently, he answers his mail while riding. I wonder why he and all other exercise bulimics peeve me so. Perhaps I'm jealous that they have the wherewithal to keep going and not quit until the joy hormones kick in.

I remember some months ago crabbing about a woman I know in the OA program who swims with religious dedication. There is also a lady in my village who makes me wild. I see her at all hours of the day and night, walking briskly from one end of the town to the other.

Why should *her* compulsion get on *my* nerves? Why do things like this upset me? Why do I care? Maybe she likes to walk. Maybe it makes her feel safe, maybe it helps her keep her weight down, so she can look in the mirror and not get nauseous. Bottom line: it's none of my business. Subconsciously, I may be trying to take the heat off *my* compulsions.

## *December 4th*

My birthday is next week. My housekeeper of thirty-two years, who knows what a baby I am about my birthday, asked me this morning what I want as a gift. I dragged her to stand beside me in front of the well-stocked larder as I took items off the shelves. I acted in silence; she kept asking impatiently what I was doing. She made it entirely clear that whatever I took I would have to put back in the right order.

"Yes, captain."

I filled my straw shopping basket with pounds of sugar, salt, rice and flour. When I had amassed thirty pounds of bags, I said: "Please, Shoshi, darling, lift the basket for me."

"It's too heavy," she replied. She didn't catch on at first and was starting to become impatient with me. She had been in the middle of doing something when I called her to the pantry.

I insisted: "Shoshi, please pick up the basket."

Again, she replied: "It's too heavy and, besides, what in God's name does this nonsense have to do with your birthday present?"

I told her: "Everything. You see, I have eight more days in order to achieve my initial weight-loss goal. I will be giving myself the removal of all thirty pounds." She loved the idea.

It was, by the way, one hell of a job to lift my straw basket with one hand. Thirty pounds is a tremendous amount of mass. I have often been naïve and blasé about this kind of drastic change. I know how easy it would be to fixate on the fact that I am still miles away from my final goal for the whole year; but in doing so, I would surely not be grateful enough for my progress.

Because I am such a hard taskmaster, such a relentless perfectionist, I didn't entirely comprehend before now what a serious accomplishment it actually is.

## *December 5th*

Yesterday I had an amazing bike ride through the city of Tel Aviv. My husband, his sister and I took the town by a storm. We got from here to there in remarkable time, reveling in the breeze. What I discovered about myself is that I am, true to nature, in hot pursuit of the perfect bike ride.

I know exactly what would constitute my bliss trip. The seat would have to be an extraordinary match to my ass, majestically supporting me. It would have to be the perfect height, so that I would at all times be in the best relationship to the pedals. The day must be full of delicious breezes–the sun must not oppress me or overwhelm my ability to see.

I would need multi-focal sunglasses in order to achieve maximal vision. Yesterday I had to make do with a cheap pair of oversized aviator frames that I plopped on over my prescription glasses.

The perfect ride has no dangerous obstacles–no little kids who are not watching where they're going, no dogs exercising freedom from the leash, no joggers, power walkers or inanimate objects like hydrants, trees and telephone poles to get in my way.

Yesterday's ride involved a level of navigational skill I have not yet mastered. I liken the event to the kinds of games children play on computers or in arcades. One must be on the alert to such an extent that with a pull of the trigger, even the sneakiest enemy can be taken down.

I was never good at things like that. I am marginally coordinated, perceptually compromised and feel somewhat unbalanced with my multi-focal glasses, never sure that I have successfully gauged the distance between me, the bicycle and the world at large.

The experience yesterday was filled with moments of delight. It was also, however, impossibly nerve-wracking. I am sure I was not even breathing much.

I tend to do that–I hold my breath when I am trying to achieve something physically precise and demanding. I used to drive Debbie, my yoga teacher, nuts with my erratic breathing. I exhaled when I was supposed to inhale, I held my breath when I was trying to master a pose. Obviously, it's asinine to hold your breath when you are exerting yourself pedaling. I guess I have to relax more, coping with whatever the universe is handing me in the way of navigational obstacles.

It may sound as if I'm on a tangent, but I don't think so. It's all part of furthering my understanding of my quest for mood perfection. Since Udel barked at me, I've become acutely aware that this preoccupation with The Ideal is even more wide-ranging than she or I realized. It beckons me to do more work on myself.

Nothing in this world will ever be perfect and this passionate quest will only frustrate me in a dramatic way. I must learn to accept that my teeth are slightly crooked, that I will always have the occasional ingrown toe nail, that my bike rides will make me sweat and pant and that the exterior of my wonderful lavender-and-green-colored car will have mud spots, peeling paint and dents. The world will never be up to my ridiculously high and improbable standards.

In order to master this change, in order to successfully rise above this lingering character defect, I am going to have to truly give myself over to my higher power. I am going to have to formulate, in utmost sincerity, a prayer that will articulate just how desperate I am to have this debilitating weakness removed. I am going to have to get on my knees and beg for this obsession with The Ideal to be taken away. Now that I know just how heinous it is, I hope it is lifted from my life sooner rather than later.

Never before have I come so close to understanding one of the most powerful dimensions of my existence. My intolerance for imperfection and flaws is glaring. It is a monster that is cutting off my air supply. As it leaves me, and I feel it going, it is more powerful than ever. I look forward to the ultimate liberation, finally rid of this cumbersome mindset.

## *December 7th*

There's a battle being waged inside my head, urging me to straighten up and fly right, urging me to indulge my unhealthy food whims. I'm not entirely sure how to resolve all this. It occupies my thoughts. I am frightened and feel like I should be way past this nonsense. I was hoping to be relieved of my preoccupation. By now, I should have been dealing with a refinement of my character and not still battling my eating addiction.

I seem to get Something from food. I wish that whatever that Something is, I could get it through other, healthier means. I wonder when the moment will manifest, that moment when this infantile banging my head against the wall will cease and I will emerge a very impressively evolved human being. This food thing is holding me back. While it provides grist for the mill, I would like to enjoy its memory and what it taught me, rather than still experience daily encounters with it.

I wish I didn't dream of my own private garden of earthly delights, where I saunter beneath trees of steaming hot pizzas, crappy candy bars from my childhood that cost a nickel, pasta dishes drowning in rich, thick sauces, every fine cookie I've ever tasted, and all the myriad goodies that have seduced me all my life.

I've just plain gotten too cocky. People have been handing me compliments and they've obviously gone to my head. All the *oohs* and *ahhs* start rolling in when there is an appreciable change in my girth. My face has been slimming down and I am beginning to look a lot better. This improvement in my appearance coincides with the enormous effort I am making to do all the right things and become the living embodiment of the Twelve Steps.

Yet I still find myself hungry, struggling with cravings. I am defiant and resentful that I have to diet in the first place. I don't like it one bit. I sense a shadow impinging on the self I prefer–the light, cheery one, the one I cherish above all others. The unresolved, complicated parts of my being are gaining on me.

As I am writing this, there are tears in my eyes; I am choked up with emotion. I have done this to myself, I have created this relationship and even though there is no life without food, I know that I have gone way too far.

## December 8th

I wandered into a minefield the other day by taking personal inventory while down in the dumps. What a colossal blunder. I had no business taking stock of my character defects while I was feeling like that. When I'm down and not my usual cheerful, peppy self, I tend to see a bloated version of my shortcomings. I exaggerate my past as one big misuse of my talents, regarding myself with a scathing eye. I am ruthless when it comes to beating myself up.

It is definitely unwise for me to go on an archeological dig into my character when I am eating crappy food, even if I'm proper with my points. It's very dangerous to assess my character traits when I'm eating a bag of popcorn instead of lunch.

## *December 10th*

They clapped for me yesterday at Weight Watchers for the pound I lost this week. While by my strict standards, it's a drop in the bucket, the truth is that it's undeniable progress. It's a testimony to the seriousness of purpose, nose to grindstone, of which I am capable.

I am ashamed to talk about this because it screams inconsistency, but since honest disclosure is the only way to recovery, I will bare all. From the get-go at Weight Watchers, I told them I didn't want to know how much I weigh. I have painstakingly and successfully avoided knowledge of these numbers for the last three months. Last night, our group leader weighed me and–in the excitement over the weight I lost–my "scorecard" slipped into view.

I'm not proud of this, but I have been wondering for the last half hour whether the number I saw was from what I weighed before or after last night's weigh-in. Good Lord, there's only a pound difference between the two numbers.

Is this really worth my time? Twenty-four pounds off is twenty-four pounds off, irrespective of the starting number.

By no means did I starve myself this week. In fact, let's not fail to acknowledge that I am carrying on a little love affair with the Skippy Chunk Style. Even this morning, rushing out of the house for a meeting, I had a teaspoon of peanut butter and half a container of diet yogurt, banana and coconut flavor. I could easily fall into the trap of daily repetitive dips into the peanut butter, topped off with creamy, delicious no-fat banana/coconut yogurt. It's happened before.

I refuse to overwhelm myself with guilt and recriminations. I must take it in stride and forgive myself. My attitude must be much more mature; I know that a day's foolishness will not put all the weight back on. I also know that a day's caprice can be dealt with calorically the next day to even the score. This is new math for me. I no longer have to be emotionally overinvested in this. The damage is not irreversible.

I am doing so much more than losing weight. As each character defect appears, I inevitably check for little signs of flexibility. I test where my attachment to this flaw might not be so rigid and steadfast. If I'm lucky and diligent, I can loosen things up and create a suitable distance between me and my attachment. I add compassion for myself and humor to the situation and often, lo and behold, I am extricated from the stranglehold of that character flaw.

## December 14th

Standing by the kitchen sink this morning, partaking in the glories of a juicy orange, I realized that despite my determination to be past this, I experience genuine feelings of guilt when I enjoy food, any food. An orange is a healthy, friendly fruit. It is a benign substance and a very low-point item. So why was I feeling like I had I no right to savor every juicy bite? What in God's name was going on? Is it possible that I don't think I deserve to enjoy food after so many years of abusing it!?

I used to fake being sick as a kid just so I could stay home to eat and watch TV. My parents were never in the house before six p.m. Until I was ten, Olga was our live-in housekeeper. She spoke English with this incredible Haitian accent. When no one was home, she spoke to me in Patois French. To this day I have great affection for that language. With Olga I laughed; around my mother, I just cowered.

I think that Olga felt sorry for me. Remember, I was a real loser back then. I couldn't even brush my own hair and get dressed for school. Even though I pretended that my smelly underpants disappeared in the hamper, I knew that she washed them and never told on me.

It wouldn't take a genius to know that food was my only sanctuary. She was only too happy to cook up tasty dishes to hoist my spirits. *She* was an eater; oh boy, was she ever. But not our food. She had her own stash, which must have gotten consumed after she did the dinner dishes. Personally, I wouldn't touch it. I thought it smelled weird.

As I sit here and write this, I have to wonder if I truly understood as a kid that this food, which I loved more than anything else in life, was altering the shape of my body. I seriously doubt that I made the connection. All I knew was that I was doing something wrong. I was being deceitful. I was lying about being sick and I was eating food I wasn't supposed to have. For that, I felt guilty. For having such a wonderful time with Olga, I felt guilty. For loving her so much more than my own mother, my conscience was heavy.

Just articulating this reminds me of an idea attributed to Freud: No one is as good or as bad as he thinks he is. I have always loved this idea. It speaks to me in an unbelievable way.

As a psychologist, listening to people's tales hours a day, I hear the overinvestment in trauma and the underinvestment in self-worth. Guilty conscience can cloud the entire personality, often leaving the individual so emotionally hamstrung that he can hardly credit himself for anything.

A hard stare in the mirror rarely yields the truth when our eyes are bespectacled with self-loathing or grandiosity.

Today, I want to enjoy my food with no accompanying feelings of fear or guilt. I want to enjoy my food without calling up ancient feelings connected to my mother and her over-involvement with my plate.

I'm finished, I'm absolutely *finished* with this part of my eating disorder. Next time I eat an orange or a juicy steak, I want to feel good, and not like I'm committing a sin. I want to eat for nutrition and pleasure and not ruin it for myself.

Am I immoral because I sometimes yearn for a treat? Am I not supposed to love eating? I *can* have a healthy enjoyment of it, as long as I don't get carried away and obsessed, or run to it to solve my problems. I suspect that if I succeed in losing fifty pounds, fair and square, slow and steady, it will be because I've discovered a fairly benign, low-point treat that thrills me time after time. Should I just eat lettuce all day? No way!

As the mathematician of my weight loss, as the chief

engineer in this construction, I have to consider all the factors. One of them is that I must enjoy doing this program and have a good time. I am not supposed to hate what I eat and resent every mouthful. To hell with that! It's my obligation to come up with creative solutions that tickle my fancy.

## *December 16th*

It's officially the holiday season; happy Hanukah to members of my club.

The gastronomics of the holiday I'm celebrating contain some of the most outrageously greasy food imaginable. There are two featured items that dominate the festivities. One is the huge fried doughnut, sans hole, filled with jelly or jam. The other greasy death trap is the potato pancake.

Over the eight days of Hanukah, I have been known to indulge myself publicly and privately. These are foods of which you don't eat just one.

This year, I'm abstaining–except in my imagination.

In my mind, I shove three ridiculously large jelly doughnuts down my gullet. My stomach is stretched and I am cruising for a bruising with the potato pancakes. One can adorn these little beauties with sour cream and salt or apple sauce and sugar.

Why choose? Have them both ways. It's a holiday.

## *December 29th*

Winter has finally arrived. I am hungrier than ever. But here's a new spin on an old routine: My husband was reading in his study. I was lying in my royal bed, watching a documentary. All of a sudden I had this thought: "I have two points coming to me." Wasting no time, I planned a strategy that would entail sneaking into the kitchen and making off with two handfuls of whole wheat challah bread. Just as I was tiptoeing past my husband, he called me into his study. I retorted, "No, no, I'm busy. I can't talk now. I'll come to you later."

"I'm onto you," he whispered. I was dumbfounded. He didn't know the specifics, but he knew enough to understand that I was in the middle of some kitchen romance.

He said: "You know, you'd feel a lot better and more successful at this endeavor if you created a mental picture of a closed kitchen till the morning. Consider the idea that you have finished eating for today."

At that moment, I felt like the archangel Michael was talking to me. I went and sat next to him. What can I say? Divine intervention. I should only be so lucky as to have this occur wherever and whenever the stupid idea hits me that I've been gypped of a couple of points and have to rectify the *situation*.

## *January 2nd*

Happy New Year, boys and girls. Here it is. I must credit myself for making some incredible strides this year. It has not been an easy undertaking by any standard. My goal is to reach a remarkable metamorphosis, one in which there is an impressive correlation between how I look and how I am. The match between my psychic self and my appearance will be obvious. To say that I yearn for this is understating a passionate desire.

Some New Year's resolutions: to stay spiritually honest

with myself and the universe, systematically slicing off any of the little scams I try to get away with. I resolve to lose another ten pounds by April 8th, Michael's birthday.

I want to wrap myself in colorful ribbons and parade around the room for his delight. Although he has been extremely gracious over the years, a silent witness to my expansions, there is no question in my mind that he will be happy for me. He's that kind of magnificent human being who would be happy to receive a birthday gift that's more about me than him.

I must admit that I didn't do myself any good on New Year's, watching a shockingly graphic documentary on drug addiction, topped off with the equally graphic Hollywood portrayal of the life of Ray Charles. I always have a problem with the explicit, unexpurgated visual accounting of addiction. Watching people out of control is a little too much for me to handle. While my workweek is an unending interaction with addicts, I only see them devoid of active participation in their vices. It would be heart-wrenching if when I looked at them, I could also see flashbacks to their desperate pursuits, their throat-grabbing irresistible urges. It would be insane if, when I looked in the mirror, I saw scenes of nasty gobbling parties in which I am out of control.

## *January 5th*

Sometimes I feel like a cheater in front of my addicts. I can "afford" the luxury of falling off the wagon; they can't. They simply cannot allow themselves the dubious sweetness or gruesome insanity of using. It's sort of not fair that

I can still eat whenever I feel like it and no one's going to call the cops on me.

*　*　*

Here it is, two and a half hours since I wrote those lines above, and I am now contemplating whether or not to cap off my "legal lunch" of cauliflower and rice with a diet oatmeal cookie.

The cookie's not the problem. It's the craving. It's upsetting that I am still struggling with this.

I am amazed by the fact that from hour to hour I can dance between two such diametrically opposed sides of myself. I can be serene and philosophical and then ridiculous.

When a craving hits, the last thing I want to do is stop in the middle, or just preceding the first bite, and say, "Lord, help me. Take this out of my hand. Take away this craving, this irresistible urge. I am begging You." But I know I must.

If I were to get wacky and succumb to the sugar temptation, I would be even more ill-equipped to field it neurologically. It is as if my brain would be being bombarded by serious toxins and it would be difficult to stop the downward spiral.

But I can do this. Even if I don't believe that the universe will deftly remove the cookie from my hand, just the mere thought of a Higher Power's intervention makes a difference. Stopping dead in my tracks, I can step back and ask myself if this is really what I mean to be doing.

Sometimes I think I need to create lines I will absolutely not cross. Other times, I think I need a *deus ex machina*, the kind with all the *Sturm und Drang* pyrotechnics of a *burning* bush. I could probably settle for my own voice, lovingly guiding me in the right direction, keeping me safe from harm.

## *January 9th*

I told my friend Eva that on her birthday in April, I would be almost skinny. This feat will necessitate fancy dancing. I have calculated the feasibility of this occurring and know it can be done–

IF…

- I continue to count no more than twenty-six points a day for the next three months
- I continue to work out on the stationary bike six days a week
- I keep a good attitude about this adventure
- I am mature about temporary setbacks
- I take this seriously and embrace the endeavor with love

On the other hand, I will fail IF…

- I let the tortured and bewildered child in me run the show
- I eat everything everyone else is eating
- I eat out of spite against the people around me or my dearly departed mother
- I tell myself that I look good enough and who cares anyway

But if things go according to plan and I reinstate my seriousness of purpose, I should be on my way.

It might seem that I am preoccupied with weight loss. I am definitely thinking about it too much, but I suppose it would be bizarre to be writing this book and oblivious to the changes in my weight. I do feel that The Weight burdening me all these years–the weight of my past, my anger, my shame, my sadness and my fears; the weight of my overblown ego, laziness, erudition and intolerance–is clearly quantifiable in pounds. I want to get rid of the last twenty-five pounds of pain and fat.

I have to give myself permission to accept the inevitable stumbles. If you take a year-long trip, there will be weather to deal with, changes in the geography, impasses and a myriad of other factors. These are the challenges you face by getting on the path in the first place. Why was I so naïve as to think that the embarkation, plus my strong determination, would be enough? When I get worked up, it never occurs to me that I might possibly fail. But failure is a stop along the way; it isn't the end of the journey.

A few days ago, I sat peacefully in the kitchen eating an orange once again. I decided to make it into an experience in mindfulness, a new-old technique designed to heighten your awareness, usually physically, at any given moment. I sectioned the orange piece by piece, segment by segment. I took a section in my hand, put it in my mouth and closed my eyes. To my utter dismay and surprise, I found that I didn't know where to begin: to take a chew on the left side or the right side of my mouth, to continue to chew or suck the juice–I just didn't know what to do. Before I could resolve all that, I swallowed the damn thing.

I said to myself, "What's with you? What's the big deal? Start again. Take another section and do it better."

## *January 11th*

My daughter, my girlfriend and my sister-in-law have all made comments about my relationship with Skippy and at one point it started to get under my skin. In defense of myself, I patiently explained that a tablespoon of peanut butter, no particular style specified, equals one Weight Watchers point. I checked my Weight Watchers point book to validate my argument and noticed that in parentheses, right beside the listing for peanut butter, it indicated how much–in grams–the portion was meant to be. It said fifteen grams. I thought to myself, "Gee, that's not very much. I wonder how much I'm eating every day without kidding myself."

Before I went to weigh the peanut butter, I called a friend to make double sure that three teaspoons equal a tablespoon. She told me that to the best of her knowledge, this is a known fact in cooking. Well, I measured out my classic teaspoon–one out of the three I would eat daily– and lo and behold! My kitchen scale was hovering between thirty and forty grams. I was horrified. I was so shocked, I measured it again.

What all this means, actually, is that I was eating something around one hundred and ten grams of peanut butter a day–that is, on a day when I wasn't defiantly dipping into the jar for extra teaspoons.

I am only allowed twenty-six points a day. If eight of them were peanut butter, but I only calculated for one point, of course I would not lose weight like I hoped to. In reality, I must have been eating close to thirty points on some days. The fact that I did this inadvertently doesn't change anything. Now that I have the knowledge, I have to act on it as a mature adult.

I tried to negotiate with the jar of Skippy, only allowing myself two teaspoons a day. Then I tried to limit my ingestion of it to three days a week. I realize now that I have to kiss this treat goodbye completely.

In order to let it go, I now have to repeat the mantra: Get over yourself, Ellie.

## *January 13<sup>th</sup>*

I haven't spoken about my relationship with the exercise bicycle in the longest time. As you know, I'm on that contraption six days a week. I can't believe I do it. I feel like I've been experiencing an upheaval of an extreme nature for six months now. Day after day, week after week, I don my bike attire and climb the stairs. I would die if anybody saw me in such a get-up. I open the shutters, check which routine I'm doing that day, put on the appropriate musical accompaniment, fill my bottle of water, strap on my pulse monitor, jump in the saddle and get riding.

In order to amuse myself, I try to beat my previous record. I'm such a competitive little overachiever. It's ironic, though, because woven into this highly disciplined routine are the more childish sides of my personality. I go into a panic when I'm sweating too much or incapable of riding fast enough.

Yesterday, after a record-breaking fifteen miles the

night before, I was a wipe-out. I was sweating like an animal and hardly had the strength to pedal quickly. My pulse was so ridiculously low, I thought I was going to faint. After twenty-five minutes I gave myself permission to dismount. Uncharacteristically, my high-achieving self let it go; I did not get overwhelmed for letting myself off the hook.

On certain subjects, I am a harsh taskmaster. But with food, I am both the con artist, cutting slack all over the place, and the whip-cracking master dieter. The lesson I hope to learn on this journey is how to moderate these jokers. That, of course, will entail making peace with them. Today I'm feeling optimistic enough to believe I will get there.

## *January 14th*

Debbie came and gave me a yoga class this morning. Lucky me! There is something new about my ability to take direction and position myself with focus and clarity of intention. As I evolve, I surrender and allow space for another thinker in my mind besides myself.

Debbie has taught me much more than yoga. She has taught me how to listen to her and how to listen to me. I am learning how to keep my mouth shut longer, interrupt less and stay with the assignment–without distracting myself with endless ruminations and obnoxious recriminations.

At the end of today's session, we did "the bowls." This is a Tibetan healing experience in which she placed a large metal bowl on my chest, which resonated for a long time after she struck it. Other humming metal bowls were strategically placed around my head.

I promised myself to pay close attention to what was going on in my mind during "the bowls." As I lay peacefully on the mat, as she struck the bowls in turn, I thought: "Oh, how lovely is that bowl on my chest? I wonder how old it is. What a lovely, light, tinkling sound is coming from that smaller bowl. I have to make sure to remember all this accurately for my journal.

"I wonder what it would be like if my compulsive gambling clients could play but never gamble? They would never win or lose money. It would just be about the fun and games. I wonder if I could bring this up when the group meets.

"Am I back on track? Can I trust myself? What's going to happen tomorrow at Weight Watchers?

"It sure is a drag to have such a fat belly. It really makes shoulder stands rather cumbersome. Maybe by the time I've lost another fifteen pounds, I will have lost this distraction.

"I really love yoga. I really love these bowls. It's so much fun to observe my thinking."

Maybe I've omitted one or two thoughts but, truly, this is as accurate a reportage as I can render. And all of this was going on when I was ostensibly relaxing! I suspect that if I were hooked up to my bio-feedback machine, it would register that indeed I was quite peaceful. I didn't, in any way, feel agitated. It was just my strange brain doing what it does.

I have decided not to chastise myself for not successfully eradicating my thoughts.

There is something very tempting to me about the idea of taking a temporary vacation from my head, from life.

Years ago, I used to fantasize about a sleep cure that I heard they did in Switzerland. There's just something about getting knocked out, being absolutely incapable of carrying on nonsensically, being in a sweet suspension and coming back weeks later full of awe and wonder, free at last from habits and torturous, self-defeating thoughts and patterns. Imagine, I go to sleep fat in winter and wake up skinny in summer.

Just because it's a silly fantasy doesn't mean I can't muse about it…

## *January 16th*

I have never mentioned another very important relationship I have in my life. Danielle–I nicknamed her Bij, short for *bijou*, French for jewel–has been a terrific friend for years. We speak daily and trade stories, comparing notes as mothers and sisters.

Danielle is ridiculously tiny. She is, in fact, the littlest grownup I know. We look laughable walking down the street together. I remember once, on a trip to Egypt, we tried to convince people we were twins.

She has a very patient ear for the trials and tribulations of my eating disorder. Even though it must be close to impossible for her to identify with it, she is compassionate and encouraging. In the years when I was purging, we would sit in her living room, watching a movie, while I downed my own pint of Ben and Jerry's. I would then ask her to freeze the movie on pause while I went to take care of the ice cream. She never batted an eyelash or begged me hysterically to mend my ways. She was always very tolerant and accepting of wherever I was at any given moment.

I, on the other hand, am always trying to fix her. I can't just love her. The same goes for my darling Eva. Something about them invites me to step in and straighten them out because *I* always know what's what. I would like to publicly declare the guilty pleasure I take in playing François Truffaut. There is no reason for them to take direction from me.

This is my amends, girls.

\* \* \*

Now that I've opened up my Pandora's Box vis-a-vis my relationship with Danielle and Eva, I am duty-bound to report a number of incidents that have occurred of late. Danielle has known, for many years, a very powerful creature named Noga.

Over the years, this Noga has amassed devotees and enemies. She is a self-styled guru with an air about her that you love to hate. I personally met her eight years ago and found her abrasive and unappealing. Her workshops offer a great deal of food for thought; she is undoubtedly intelligent and experienced. She is clearly a force to be reckoned with, but I opt to keep my distance and learn my lessons from more humble and soft guru types.

Danielle has, in these last few months, been in very close proximity to Noga. She has been to various seminars, each time coming back and extolling the virtues of Noga the Great. Every time Danielle tries to ram this down my throat, I bristle. I ask what exactly Noga has done to deserve this level of deification. Let's not forget that Noga has created her life with no husband, no children, no job except spouting words of wisdom, mostly in the realm of the theoretical. It's easier to rattle off insights when very little is claiming your attention.

This morning, an interesting thing occurred between me and Danielle. I called her to tell her how lousy I was feeling, what a bad night I'd had, what obnoxious dreams plagued my sleep and what an overwhelming feeling of despair and harsh self-criticism I was experiencing. I told her in these words: "I have been doing everything in my power to become a pure individual. I have tried systematically to eliminate every character defect that weighs me down. I have tenaciously clung to a program of self-denial and discipline. I try so passionately to become the purest version of myself."

What does she hand me at 8:15 on a Sunday morning?

"There are no pure people except Noga. Noga is the only pure person I know."

I have no nerves for the likes of another Noga lecture and I tell her to please spare me the Noga. I'm in no shape to even be aggressive.

I get off the phone and decide that a bike ride will help. I don my bike costume; I force myself to mount the stairs to my exercise room. All of a sudden, I understand why I cannot bear to deal with the Noga thing. I run back down to my bedroom, pick up the phone and yell in Danielle's ear: "I am pissed at you! I just realized why I get so aggravated about Noga. It's because I'm so fucking jealous. I'm jealous for a multiplicity of reasons. Want me to share my insights?"

"Yes, of course. I can't wait. I'm so proud of you."

"If you laugh, I'll come over there and give you a smack."

"I am listening, Ellie, with a big smile on my face. Please tell me what you've discovered."

"Here it comes: A. She is so important to you. B. She can tell you what's what, like I do, but she never annoys you and I'll bet she never feels guilty for trying to control you. C. She must have achieved an impressive amount of spiritual recovery, and I feel so much today like I am lagging behind, coming in last in the enlightenment marathon."

As I said C, I was choking back my tears, hardly able to pronounce "marathon." Before I could break out in convulsive sobs, Danielle started laughing into the receiver. In an instant, I saw the comedy and joined in.

Danielle and I were both laughing at my honest self-disclosure; we both felt relieved. Seeing beyond resentments and 'fessing up to my truth is painful, yet incredibly liberating. I am so grateful to God that my truth is being revealed to me as I can face it.

Even though I feel like I am still light years away from bona fide self-actualization, I think I'm pointed in the right direction.

No, I don't *think* I am; I know I am.

## January 19*th*

My older son, my most staunch mirror on planet earth, whom I happen to love dearly, has informed me that he has a theory about my heavily-accented Hebrew. He maintains that I have deliberately kept New York in my Hebrew in order to make a statement: I am a New Yorker, not an Israeli. I am not one of you; you wish you were like me.

I am not jubilant when I get criticized. I am defensive. Maybe I should *not* still have New York in my Hebrew, after four decades in Israel. It's as if I am being accused of deliberately holding onto this accent for dear life. He we are again, my firstborn and I locking horns. He is trying to uncover a truth, or a version of reality as he sees it, and I can't bear the humiliation, the accusation that I am a faker.

Righteous indignation seeped from my pores as I tried to explain to him all the neurological and psycho-linguistic reasons that I sound like I do. I explained about brain plasticity and how, after adolescence, language must be learned methodically and not absorbed by simple exposure—as it is with kids. The same goes for accents. They are almost impossible to mimic when you learn a language later in life. I even managed to slip in the fact that two months after I got here, I became pregnant with him and was so bilious, I couldn't commit myself to studying Hebrew properly. I had to settle for private lessons and did the best I could.

It's thirty-six hours later and I know that some of what he said is one hundred percent true. I am unique, I have always been unique and I pride myself on this. I have an ego investment in not acculturating here. I do like to stand apart from Israelis. As much as I wish I could be accentless and impeccable in Hebrew grammar, I'm sort of glad that I'm not.

## *January 22nd*

It was on this day forty-one years ago that I stood under a bridal canopy in a wedding hall in downtown Tel Aviv.

My close family all flew over from New York to witness the event. My husband designed my wedding dress. It was a very tailored gown, a statement on the art of simplicity.

I was tempted to put it on today just for fun, but realizing it would only be a powerful humiliation, I held myself back. Even though curiosity often rules me (under the guise of scientific inquiry), I know that I can surely not even slip my arm into that fitted, white silk sleeve. The changes in my bosom, midriff, back and belly are undeniable. I am forty pounds heavier than I was on my wedding day. While my face is deceptively slim, it will take a Herculean effort to get my body to cooperate with the dress.

It's funny about me, with the curiosity thing. Sometimes I yearn for graphic proof of just how far astray I've gone or just how much trimmer I'm becoming. At least today I did the smart thing and kept myself in ignorance.

## *January 24th*

I caught a glimpse of another *The Biggest Loser* rerun last night on the TV and it set me to thinking. There was a woman on the show who had lost sixty pounds in three months! I've lost barely half that in *seven* months. Now, I'll give you that she is exercising with a coach many hours a day. She is also, I'm assuming, eating like a bird. It's not fair. Anyway, I am still wrestling with the poor Little Ellie inside and she weighs a lot more than I do.

Haven't I successfully weaned things out of my life? I haven't had a cigarette in years. While I was never a heavy smoker, I still loved my frosty glass of Diet Coke and

Marlboro to greet the day. It was a ritual I treasured, even on blustery winter mornings. What can I say, I loved it.

So here I am without cigarettes or daytime TV, and I'm counting food points. How much deprivation must I expose myself to?

Gradually, I am getting better. I less frequently crave the escape that cookies and television have always provided. I less often want to stare for hours at idiotic situations, played by hardly impressive actors.

When you need television for the reasons I have sought it out, you tend to be an indiscriminate viewer, finding tolerable entertainment in a hardly impressive milieu. I got hooked for years on a soap opera, breathlessly arriving in my driveway by four o'clock in the afternoon whenever I could. I even had endless conversations with one of my nieces about the characters and what they were up to. I finally turned to my higher power to free me from my attachment to this show. I now only watch it occasionally.

## *January 25th*

Over lunch yesterday, my husband asked me to talk about why historically, I have had so much trouble committing to a food plan and sticking to it. I told him that I think it has to do with bravery. I explained that for me to *not* eat something I want, for me to *not* say: "Oh, the hell with it, who cares if I eat a whole pita?" is an act of courage. This might sound insane as a description of bravery, but I know it is true.

Maybe it's like that with addicts, especially in recovery. They don't very much want their addiction in their face. I would not advise my students who struggle with a gambling addiction to spend a weekend in Vegas. It would require an unnecessary test of bravery.

Food is, of course, another matter. I am never going to get away from the pitas of this world. So, with each encounter, my bravery is being tested.

## *January 27th*

I saw something on TV the other night that blew my brains out: a ten-year-old documentary on competitive eating. God Almighty, this was outrageous. The film followed a British competitive eater as he readied himself for a Fourth of July food competition in Coney Island. You guessed it: the food contest involved the downing of Nathan's hot-dogs. This guy traveled to Japan to get gobbling techniques from a master swallower.

The young Japanese man was a slim yet muscle-bound eater who eventually won the Coney Island contest by downing forty-eight dogs and buns in twelve minutes. The dogs, apparently, were the easy part. The buns required some fancy interventions. His secret was moistening them.

I loved watching this. I was screaming with laughter. It was insane, though very, very interesting for me as a compulsive overeater. I must say that watching people wolf down outrageous amounts in the shortest period of time was a little too close for comfort. The only difference between me and them is they are handsomely rewarded and I just get fat.

## *January 29th*

Part of my pseudo-Amazonian self-view is dictated by the fact that in my first school years, I was so much larger than my peers. My peculiar growth spurt right after my eyes were operated on, the physiological explanation for which has never been clear to me, meant that when I was about eight years old, I looked at least fourteen. An eight-year-old is not supposed to look like an adolescent in full bloom. No one ever believed that I was telling the truth about my age.

Today I look younger, if anything, than my years. I have a very youthful nature and I dress more like a young woman than I do like a dowdy, middle-aged creature.

Let's imagine that I keep doing the right things for the next eight or nine months and the inevitable happens: the fat evaporates, poof, like it's gone up in smoke. There are no traces. Only my skeleton and organs remain, covered beautifully in all the rest of my anatomy sans the blubber suit. Voilà! I am a perfect size eight.

I say "perfect" and the little voices in my inner Greek chorus sing: "Size eight, my dear, but never perfect." Of course, my perfection-obsession ruins everything because, invariably, even when I am a size eight, I might have a hangnail, bloating or a hundred million other flaws in my psycho-physiology.

But damn it! That should not detract from the fact that I would be a size eight and would have to get rid of the clothes I've worn as an eighteen. Size eight is a new story. I don't think I've worn a size eight since I *was* eight. By the age of ten, I was already five-foot-six with a very present bosom and a shoe size that was hardly attainable at the local bootery.

I am used to being a big, handsome gal. I have never been small. On me, size eight will be small. Just sitting here trying to visualize it has me vibrating between panic and incredulity. The intellectual part of my mind cannot accurately conjure up the picture of a miniaturized me. The emotional side is seriously anxious.

I have to explore this.

All my life, I thought the thing I most wanted from the universe was to be thin. If I could just be thin, everything would be perfect. If I just looked normal in a bathing suit or shorts, I wouldn't have a care in the world. Today I know that that kind of thinking was ridiculous. What a dumbbell idea. And to have clung to it for so long! It's incomprehensible to me that this thinking ruled me so profoundly.

But the possibility now exists that I could, in less than a year, become my dream size.

What then?

Let's face it. I am never going to be a twenty-year-old wearing a size eight. I am going to be a slimmed down version of my middle-aged self. There will be bulges and sagging skin all over my body—that's a given. It makes me sad. I think it also makes me angry that it's taken me this long to grow up and let go of the baby fat. My bad luck. I've awakened from my psychic slumber and decided to grow up and take care of this problem just as I'm reaching the irreversible.

Imagine instead that I don't fully reach my ideal until I'm eighty years old. Wouldn't this be a cruel and delicious irony? I actually delight in the idea. It would serve me right. I am smiling as I say this. There I'll be, a slim, blue-haired grandmother, making weekly visits to a beauty parlor so that I can be pampered. I haven't been pampered in years, but maybe by then, I won't have the strength and stamina to jazz myself up alone.

The prospect of getting old and decrepit gives me the willies. I don't want to become a burden on my family or dependent on the kindness of strangers. Oh sweet universe, only You know your plan for me and if it is in Your heart to see me through to happy endings, I will gladly go. Secretly, I believe that none of these details will mean a thing in the long run. Death will be full of terrific surprises, an end to suffering and the entrance to bliss.

For now, I think I am best doing the "one day at a time" program and not overinvesting myself in philosophical conjecture.

## *February 1$^{st}$*

Since I'm so conflicted about movement and strenuous exercise, it should come as no surprise to you that I continue to *not* have a ball six days a week on that bike upstairs. I'm already kind of cranky when I strap my feet onto the damn thing. I hope every time that my brain chemistry will finally give me the supreme gift of joy, when the endorphins are released and the serotonin is taken up.

When I've ridden thirty minutes or so and I'm huffing and puffing, I inevitably entertain the thought that maybe this time, just once, I won't ride for forty-two minutes. Thirty minutes will be good enough.

I don't want to be a cheater. I don't want to be a big, fat baby who keeps giving herself little dispensations. I want to be a big girl who can meet this challenge day after day and turn it into a good experience.

Dreading it, figuring how I can weasel out of it, doesn't make me feel good about myself. It makes me feel like I'm failing myself, short-changing my spiritual growth and ripping myself off.

Today when I finish this writing session, I am going to face my bicycle with a whole new attitude. This is a commitment I am making. I am going to mount that bike with such joy and anticipation, knowing it is a friendly and safe means to an end.

## *February 4$^{th}$*

We had a wonderful meeting yesterday at Weight Watchers. Our group leader Ziv is so terrifically prepared each week. Dedicated to our success, she is full of new ideas and innovations. Last night she brought a highly decorated box with a slit through which to put our estimation of how much weight we will lose in the next eight weeks, in time for Passover.

I wrote on my slip of paper that by the time I sing "When We Were Slaves in the Land of Egypt," I will be ten pounds lighter, bringing me to a total of thirty-five. I am going to do what I can to honor my pledge.

As I stepped gingerly on the scale last night, Ziv's face lit up and she said, "Good job, Ellie." She was genuinely happy for me because I had lost close to two pounds and was starting to get somewhere after a month of very slow progress.

Another thing she had us do last night was close our eyes and cooperate with a little experiment. She was very cautious and sensitive about the fact that perhaps there were people in the room who wouldn't "go for" this type of activity. With a kind of New Age spiritual sound on the CD player, she asked us to pick a future date and visualize how we would look on that day.

I have been working with visualizations for most of my life and was having a ball with her instructions. Almost invariably, I am the teacher. It was fun to be a student for a change and allow another thinker some space in my mind.

I conjured up the forthcoming reunion at Scarsdale High in October. By the way, this date marks the projected completion of this book. I have given five seasons to the task of liberating myself from the status of "fat girl." What could be more appropriate than commemorating this milestone at my high school reunion?

In my visualization, I saw myself nine months from now in a lavender-colored wool sweater, a spectacular hue. Just visualizing the color made me start to cry. It was a well-fitted garment that gave me a terrific upper body. My trousers were a tailored gray affair. My hair was in a long silver pony tail–I haven't dyed my hair in years. I imagined all my old friends passing out when they saw me. The consensus was: "Oh, my God, Ellie, you haven't changed a bit."

Yeah, right. Who had grey hair in high school?

I need to cherish this fantasy and actualize it. It is definitely within my grasp. But be warned, it's only in my grasp if I continue to hold it precious and do everything in my power to contribute to its birth. It's physically possible to achieve, but the big question here is if my spirit and emotions will support my greater good or sabotage it.

## *February 11th*

At Weight Watchers yesterday, I found that I had lost another pound. I was a little pissed off because a woman in the group who has been there only half the amount of time has lost twice as much as I have. She explained that her secret is eating a lot less than the prescribed number of points.

She whispered to me that she was terribly hungry. Who wouldn't be? Hell, I am in this for the long haul. If I wanted to go on a crash diet, I would have gone off carbs again. I am jealous of her fifty-pound weight loss, but I know that mine is the better way. Slowly, I am learning a new sensibility about food. I am getting to know my needs and desires. Over time, I am becoming familiar with the difference between physical hunger and the psychological kind. Very subtly, I am reaching a point where I can stop myself before I do the regrettable. I owe all of this progress to my spiritual expansion and the ever-deepening humility that is emerging.

Before I give myself too many compliments and gold medals for sanity, I would like to describe my latest dip. On Monday, all my groups were unexpectedly cancelled and I had, all of a sudden, a lot of free time on my hands. I thought, "Oh, goodie, I am going to use my time well. I have so much reading to catch up on. This is going to be great."

It was one in the afternoon when I settled in bed to continue reading Amos Oz's wonderful book, *A Tale of Love and Darkness*. The English translation is superb and not stilted like they often can be. I truly savor the sentences. Oz takes me to an interesting Israel in the 1940s.

I adore reading in bed. Unfortunately, I also adore watching TV in bed.

Eleven months ago, I made a pledge to avoid daytime TV like the plague. I have almost exclusively honored my vow, but, well... Two days ago, I tumbled into the netherworld of daytime TV again. Lord, have mercy. My husband saved me from myself a little by finally interrupting and suggesting a long walk by the beach in Tel Aviv. It was just what the doctor ordered.

*February 12th*

In an effort to enrich my understanding of myself, I decided to take a Bach Flower Remedy. I have been working with this particular alternative medical approach for the last three decades. I have personally experimented with many different flowers, but never have I tried this one before.

The flower is called Agrimony. You give it to very cheerful people who have managed to keep their pain under wraps—often, they are not even aware of it themselves.

I knew I needed this, but I failed to imagine how difficult the journey would be.

I, as you must have gathered, have reinvented myself a number of times since my pained childhood. By fifteen, I was already unforgettable. Ask anyone who went to high school with me and they'll tell you who Ellie was—a cross between Bette Midler and Groucho Marx.

If you want to have a good time, you want to be with me. I have a contagious, fun spirit. But it's an invention. I had to invent myself at several serious crossroads. In order not to feel pain or, God forbid, convey it, I became the larger than life, mythological Ellie.

Historically, whatever pain snuck in and reared its ugly head was quickly vanquished with food. That did the trick for decades. But since walking into Overeaters Anonymous, I started to confront the whole constellation of compulsive overeating. I could no longer enjoy the "benefits" of food in the same way again.

Maybe Agrimony will help me face my feelings instead of eating over them.

## *February 15$^{th}$*

I just marched into the office of Dr. Diana, my favorite women's health professional, after a fourteen-month hiatus. I know that it's not good to wait so long between appointments but I think part of me wanted to be able to show her how much weight I had lost. She knows that food and I have been sworn enemies since forever.

Normally, I am loath to step on her scale. But this time I jumped on it, thinking I was going to wow her with my impressive weight loss.

"Good work, Ellie. You lost fifteen pounds."

"Fifteen pounds, Diana? What are you talking about? I've lost more than twenty-five."

"It pains me to tell you that according to this scale, you haven't."

"It can't be. I get weighed every week at Weight Watchers."

"My only explanation is that since we last met, you managed to gain a lot of weight, which you then lost. But compared to what you weighed over a year ago, you're only, and I don't say this lightly, fifteen pounds thinner. You should only know, Ellie—you look a lot better."

I left her office with a stiff smile on my face, wanting to get the hell out of there as fast as possible. Even though she explained everything so logically, I couldn't bear to hear the facts.

The Agrimony I've been taking has been dissolving my mask of cheerfulness-no-matter-what. Without my usual brave face, I fell apart. I ended up canceling the whole rest of the day. In a profoundly uncharacteristic move, I took a bath at two in the afternoon, then donned my nightgown and got into bed.

The garb ensured that I was not going to be riding my exercise bicycle or leaving the house to go to Weight Watchers. I put off the addicts group I always give on Tuesdays because I knew that, at this point, I could not render what they needed. I had to attend to myself in whatever manner I could find.

My first instinct was of course to have a private food festival; I had plenty of free time and no one was around. I contemplated the "ifs" for a while, practically driving myself nuts.

At some point in this craziness, I said: "Stop it. Are you seriously going to let this 'realization' drive you mad? Ruin your day? Affect you to such a degree? Ellie, calm down."

It dawned on me that the best way to use this moment of clarity was to write down my thoughts and feelings.

At the top of the page I wrote: "All the time wasted, all the missed opportunities." I decided to tackle this by listing some of my character defects. They provide the powerful material that keeps me from being the most refined version of myself. I took a deep breath and put my shame and pride aside. Here is the list I composed. It explains how I've sabotaged myself time after time:

Silliness

Stupidity

Stubbornness

Immaturity

Selfishness

Hypocrisy

Self-righteousness

Righteous indignation

Phoniness

This is, I guess, a partial list, a condensed version of saboteurs. I conjure up these horrible devices in order to live with my existential emptiness, anger, sadness, fear and frustration. It might be occurring to you now that there must be a contradiction: How could I possibly be such a marvelous, fun person with all of these foul character traits? The answer is simple. Most of these traits are hidden behind the mask. Unless you happen to be under my skin, you wouldn't know about them. Hell, I hardly know about them myself.

I guess my nearest and dearest have all been, at some point in time, affected by my glaring weaknesses. But they have also basked in the brighter sunshine of my effervescent being and forgiven me. My light is much brighter than anything else about me.

As I write this and think about it, I am gladdened by the idea that the logical consequence of my maturation is that I will no longer have infantile needs. This excites me, for if the truth be told, one of my strongest secret longings is to be someone's beautiful little baby daughter.

Perhaps what I long for is to experience adoration with nothing expected of me—no demands, no disappointments.

## *February 17$^{th}$*

On my way to work the other day, I decided not to bring candy like I usually do. I felt that the group counted on me to be Santa Claus three times a week and decided that I was beginning to feel resentful. I knew in my heart that they loved me and that I was not buying their affections with my treats; yet maybe, from my side of things, I was being a people-pleaser.

I volleyed this argument back and forth in my head. In the end, I decided to buy sixteen packages of chocolate nonsense. Once they were all consumed, a new, treat-free era would begin at the meetings. I even shared this with the group when I got there. I invited them to take a journey into the depths of my "conflict" and my need to work on feeling more secure. It's childish to need everybody's love at all costs.

The room is peopled by addicts of all sizes and shapes. Their addictions are gruesome and have taken them to darkness I only know in my imagination. For them, this candy is a little diversion, a little fun, sweet activity to uplift their spirits.

One gal in the room, a beautiful young alcoholic, said to me: "Ellie, this bringing of chocolate each week that you do has always been hard for me to understand. You are abstinent from it, you never partake of it in front of us, but we know it is your poison, to be avoided like the plague. Can you imagine me bringing liquor to the group? Ellie, I'm glad that you've decided to stop doing this. It's not good for you; it's not good for us. It just perpetuates the craziness."

She was right. Besides, I don't need to be the reason why a room full of addicts is stuffing fistfuls of melting chocolate into their pockets for later. What was I thinking?

## *February 20th*

I showed up at Weight Watchers last night. Ziv, my precious counselor, was weighing someone as I slipped into the room. She whispered, and I quote: "Where have you been? I missed you. Is everything OK?"

What a reception. What a way to greet a person who simply missed one meeting. It's a testimony to what a sensitive human being she is. Throughout these months, overseeing this adventure, she has shown so much tenderness and sympathy for me and my journey.

I was one of the last members to be weighed: no change. It's OK, though. I had no grandiose expectations. I know that part of my challenge is to get over some expansive psychological hurdles. If this were easy, it would be rather meaningless spiritually. It is grist for my mill. I am actually a very grateful compulsive overeater and I reiterate: had it not been for my frustration at being overweight, I would never have gone to Overeaters Anonymous. I would never have had a chance to taste the Twelve Steps and savor their sweetness.

## February 22<sup>nd</sup>

Woke up in such a state of joy and hope. Gratitude was oozing from every cell of my being and I could barely contain my happiness. Plans kept changing and I saw each one as a fantastic opportunity to have an even better experience than I had previously anticipated.

It was one of those spring-in-winter days that lifts everybody's spirits. The mood in the air was significantly optimistic. All my kids at the rehab (some of them are in their forties and fifties) were also more lighthearted than usual. I used this fact as a springboard to plunge into the topic of good mood insurance. I am like a dog with a bone: I will never give up my role as cheerleader for the cause of good mood and enthusiasm. I am always on the prowl for more sane and safe items to add to my stockpile of mood insurance techniques.

One of the patients insisted on having her puppy in her lap during the group session. For the most part, the puppy was sleeping and completely inactive. I thought I would melt looking at this scene. I was dying to have a chance with that darling creature. I could only imagine how relaxed that puppy was. At one juncture, when this young lady started to share excitedly, the little puppy lifted his head, opened his eyes, looked around, saw he wasn't in any danger and proceeded to doze off again.

This struck me as so thoroughly sweet and innocent that I decided to add the idea of a dozing puppy to my list of guaranteed mood ensurers. Here's the trick with mood ensurers: you must be sure to remember to use them.

Throughout most of my adult life, I have been in

a permanent state of exuberance and *chutzpah*. If I was depressed, except for that bad year before I learned how to meditate, I didn't notice. I was kind of happy and cheerful all the time. When I wasn't, it was in reaction to something upsetting that happened externally. I did not have mood swings. Yes, on the days of my ovulations and pre-period, I was given to extremes of emotionalism and nostalgia. But the rest of the time, I most emphatically was not a moody person. Until peri-menopause hit me, I was lucky enough to be even-tempered and cheerful.

Today, my moods rule the whole of my being and I cannot remotely play oblivious to them. They sneak up on me, they grab me by the throat, make things fabulous and catastrophic. That is why, I guess, losing weight today is so much harder than: "I can do this, this is in my realm, what a fabulous challenge, I'm going to have a ball doing this, just you wait."

All that Ellie-cheerleader-type resolve feels out of reach when my mood gets compromised—and I'm not motivated to stretch myself and get it back in hand. I can wake up ready to take on all challenges, field all blows. In this frame of mind, I eat like a doll. If a sad mood stages a surprise attack, the effort suddenly weighs on me. I don't want to *have to* resist temptation—or to give in to it. I'd rather my brain didn't tempt me with crazy comfort cravings in the first place.

## *March 22<sup>nd</sup>*

Dear Diary, it has been one month to the day since I've had an opportunity to share my thoughts with you. For two weeks I was ill and unable to come to work; for two more weeks, I was abroad and geographically distanced from this experience. A day didn't go by that I wasn't thinking about how much I missed writing.

At the beginning of my stay in San Francisco, I was an impressive eater. I amazed myself. I consistently made sane gastronomic choices.

Unfortunately, my composure went out the window at the airport, where they wouldn't let me do curbside check-in because I had a one-way ticket. I was whisked into the terminal and placed in a special security isolation area. No one would speak to me. They told me to face the wall.

After a full-body search and a machine that shot puffs of air at me, I was allowed to go to the gate. I had an hour and a half to kill, so naturally I took stock of my food options.

I began with a very mature and gentle selection of steamed vegetables. Since I was such a champ, I figured I was good for a few extra bonus points. I deliberated and somehow couldn't find the wherewithal to ask my Higher Power for help, so I wound up buying an oat bran muffin. I lied to myself, saying, "I'll only have a few nibbles." By the time I finished the muffin, I was eyeing a package of peanut butter M&Ms.

I sat myself down with a copy of *USA Today*–my way of keeping abreast with American culture after such a long hiatus–and the bag of goodies.

Obviously, the universe was with me as M after M kept falling to the floor as if they were magnetized to it.

It was quite funny. I had to throw out more than I could throw down my gullet.

Obviously, nobody in the terminal gave a damn about me, but I guess the sugar from the muffin and the candy started to make me feel too conspicuous and a little paranoid. Along with guilt–I hadn't had a slip like that in months–I felt a surge of energy and committed myself to a twenty-minute, non-stop, exhausting walk round and round the terminal. It was my half-assed attempt at burning off some of the unwanted calories.

I boarded the plane. To my dismay, I found myself wedged between two young men in very tight quarters; economy class is designed to pack the most people in per inch. It is humiliating and uncomfortable. I lead a very non-luxurious life, but when it comes to airplane travel, I am a hopeless princess.

There I was, jammed in between these fellows, and the lady came by and asked if any of us wanted a cold beverage. I asked her if they served little snacks, because by then my appetite alarm was buzzing and anything would do. By my third, tiny-sized, airline excuse for a bag of pretzels, the guy on my right was shuddering. He put his hand over his mouth and nose to shield himself from whatever he might catch from me. The guy on my left rolled his eyes and told the stewardess to stop feeding the *meshuganeh*.

\* \* \*

Now in L.A., I find myself deliberately testing my friend Ruthie, baiting her, setting her up to dare to intercede. She is amazing. She lets me play out this insanity with very little intervention. A few times, she has asked me if I'm all right with what I am doing. She even asked me once if I felt OK that she wasn't trying to protect me from myself.

I played with the food sanity boundaries for close to four days. No, I did not gain back twenty pounds. It's not about that. Yes, I have been back on track for the last ten days, but I cannot stop wondering what got into me. It was as if I wanted desperately to discredit myself; as if I wanted to show everyone how far I have not yet come, how unstable and shaky my recovery is, how human I still am.

But as I sit here writing this, I know that after eight months of Weight Watchers and the exercise bicycle and this blessed memoir, not to mention OA, I have learned so much about myself and my eating that I would be hard-pressed to imagine it is all for naught. I prefer to think that this has been a lone incident of acting out, an attempt to cope with coming back to America after a year.

I have never explored the experience in this book, but I must say that living in Israel for more than half my life makes my visits to America complicated. Many of my relationships in the United States are ancient ties. Between family and friends, I am attached to scores of wonderful people who know me and love me. While I adore being with most of them, I often feel pressed to close the gap of the long months that have separated us. I sing and dance at high speed to catch everyone up on my life; the good times, the bad times—I don't want them to miss a drop.

You might be wondering what all this has to do with my overeating. Maybe nothing, maybe everything. Catching up in the continental United States is intrinsically different from catching up with a friend in Israel with whom I've lost touch for a year. America is just different for me—altogether familiar and foreign at the same time. America is mother tongue, motherland, but might as well be in another galaxy.

## March 25$^{th}$

My husband has a sister, Tova, whom I consider one of my most valuable friends. It is she who invited me on the Weight Watchers journey. I owe her for this.

Tova is one of my role models. I wonder what she would say if she knew. She is a rather shy woman, eight years my junior, who is given to frequent sparks of down-to-earth wisdom, which I often sorely need.

In Tova's year with Weight Watchers, she has slowly but surely succeeded in completely metamorphosing herself. She started out a rather bulky gal and has turned into a graceful, sculptured, sylph-like version of herself, fifty pounds lighter. She did it so reliably, week after week. Taking the job seriously, she managed to achieve this with no drama whatsoever.

There are huge stylistic differences between us. First of all, Tova is the most levelheaded, sane person I know. She is solid and accomplished. She is rarely overwhelmed by anything. I suspect this is primarily due to the fact that she is not neurotic. She is not overinvested in her emotions.

She is a very scientific and mathematical person who excels in the physical and intellectual world. Among other things, she is a remarkable cook and gardener.

I am some kind of ridiculous blend of science and art. I am as emotional as I am intellectual. I am passionate and, as much as I hate to admit it, neurotic. My emotions get in the way, my moods rule; I am tripped up by my character weaknesses. Tova is a doer. I am a thinker and a talker. I talk about losing weight. I talk to everybody about losing weight.

Tova would never in her life talk to a stranger about her weight.

I ask myself—why do I glorify Tova? Why do I think of her as the last word in mental stability? How sane is it that she became fifty pounds overweight? How sane is it that in my long relationship with her, she has gone up and down the scale on countless occasions?

The essential difference between Tova and me is that she does not wrestle with herself. When she's in a period of overeating, she eats too much and goes with it. When she's on a diet, she goes with that.

When I'm in either of those circumstances—eating or dieting—it's a constant media frenzy. I tell everybody about my successes and failures. I overindulge in self-pity when I'm binging and crave attention when I am dieting. My ups and downs are aired publicly. Hers are never discussed.

We went on a Sabbath afternoon walk yesterday—Tova, her brother my precious husband, and I. Every other block, I was either *kvetching* about how hard it was for me to keep up or praising myself for walking so long. I had a comment about everything. I was so overly self-reflective, so impossibly self-examined. The truth is, who gives a damn whether some stretch of a walk is harder or easier for me? I still need to comment, need to invite witnesses to my evolution. I wonder what it would be like to outgrow this nonsense.

## March 26$^{th}$

I would be lying if I tried to give the impression that I have overcome the entire constellation called "compulsive overeating." I haven't entirely mastered this yet. It does feel like I'm getting closer to where I want to be as a human being, not just a number on the scale. I'm more often than not making good choices, the kinds of choices that nurture my greater good.

I wonder how it is that when I want to do something in life–to get from here to there–I just do it, right? I don't interfere with the act, I don't over-think it, I don't get emotional about it; I just do it.

If I want to go from the first floor to the second floor, I mount the stairs and voilà! I have just accomplished my desire. I have given action to a thought. If my dishes are piling up in the sink, I get up and wash them. I inevitably feel better after doing it. I feel a sense of power–I have some say in the way my world is ordered and I feel very good about myself. There is no emotion that stands in my way, preventing me from actualizing my desire to tidy up. The only emotion, if any, is the resounding sense of satisfaction over a job well done.

I was sitting in the kitchen two hours ago, after Pilates, eating a delicious, well-balanced breakfast. My food was tasty and filling and absolutely low in points. As I finished it, I caught myself thinking: "This was great and hardly three points. I am going to have this whole breakfast all over again.

"Are you nuts–what's the matter with you? You just ate a full breakfast. Who cares if it was only three points?

You're ahead of the game. Besides for which, it's entirely conceivable that if you eat this breakfast all over again, it won't be as novel, tasty and filling as it was the first time. What's your problem?"

I settled for a few Swedish crackers and butter. I gave this to myself as a little gift for not eating the entire breakfast again.

## March 28<sup>th</sup>

I had another glorious session with Isella yesterday. Since November, what began as massage therapy blossomed into a bi-monthly session of somatic experience. I would be hard-pressed to define it and limit it; that would not be fair. Basically, she conducts our hour and fifteen minutes together with me talking, almost always with my eyes closed, identifying where in my body I am experiencing anger, sadness, loneliness, emptiness and, very often, *verguenza*–shame in Spanish. My Isella was born in Uruguay and I love to throw Spanish phrases and assorted vocabulary into our meetings.

Yes, it's *verguenza* that seems to accurately portray a lifetime of repressed emotion. Through my work with her, I have come to understand the degree to which I separate my mind from my body. The shame of being a cockeyed little girl with a plastic eye patch; the shame of being so much taller and heftier than the kids my age; the shame of having been tampered with sexually; these were the early trappings of a human being who was about chop off her head with a machete.

Before I began working with Isella, I had almost no idea

where in my body I was holding any emotion. Knowledge of that sort did not come easy. At first I thought she was kidding; how in God's name was I to identify what emotion I was having in some part of my cheek, finger, or chest? It was another language, another culture, this therapeutic exchange we had. She has gotten me in touch on such a deep level with regret and animosity. For this moment in my personal journey, I feel confident that this kind of work is exactly what I need.

## March 29th

Years ago, I was working on a book about the psychological ramifications of disfigurement. This subject holds a great fascination for me. I am deeply intrigued by how people go on living productive and fruitful lives with all the staring and pity.

Staring, disgust, and pity are also part of the experience of having an eating disorder, at least the obvious ones like obesity or anorexia. I am always conscious, however, of the different quality of stares directed at people who have been handicapped by their own hands.

If my hands had not shoved too much food in my mouth, I would never have become fat in the first place. My weight problem, on a strictly physical level, is due solely to an act my hands perform countless times a day. When a person looks at a fat little girl or obese young man, they know that the human being in front of them can't control the hands that are feeding the mouth.

The reasons for the hand-mouth excesses don't matter much. The psychological underpinnings don't make a damn bit of difference. When you look at a fat person, you only see the result of the excess eating and not the pain that caused it.

I am not suggesting that the next time you see a mountainous creature waddling down the street you burst into tears of compassion. Don't lock eyes with an obese stranger and explain how you understand that life must have been so overwhelming, leaving no other recourse but interminable face-stuffing. Don't go out of your way to tell a heavyset person that he should forgive himself for failing so miserably to deal with life on its own terms, resorting to the overeating that just makes him fatter.

If your eyes can't take in what you're looking at when a skeletal or whale-like creature passes through your visual field, simply remember that this *creature* deserves just as much love as the conventional handicapped person.

## *April 5th*

The other night at the Seder, I wore my mother's amethyst and diamond necklace. The necklace was her signature piece. Now it is in my possession and I intend to do right by it.

My mom exclusively wore stockings and high heels. She was meticulously coiffed and groomed, like other dignified women of her era. Boy, did that gal have poise and charm.

I have to tell you, at this very moment I look like nothing even vaguely reminiscent of my precious mother. She wouldn't know whether to laugh or cry if she saw my get-up.

I am wearing ankle boots, grossly out of style, with socks protruding from the rim of the boot. The socks are silly and loudly colorful. I am wearing yoga tights and huge, klutzy underpants that no self-respecting woman would be caught dead in.

I have to start a new paragraph about the brassiere I'm wearing. In New York, in a desperate mad dash at Lane Bryant on a Sunday morning, I purchased two purple brassieres. Except for the color and the price, nothing was right. These brassieres would fit a two-hundred-and-fifty-pound woman nicely. By the grace of God, I weigh tons less than that. I look so ridiculous in them. They make me busty and comical. My husband said this morning that they do nothing for me; what an understatement for this silly undergarment.

I am wearing a long-sleeved purple cotton T-shirt whose color absolutely thrills me, but other than that, there isn't anything stylish about it. My mother wouldn't even go to sleep in it if she were freezing.

The crowning glory of my look is my long, straight, natural-colored hair. People comment about it a lot as it looks like I've spent hours getting it streaked. I've been wearing it in a pony-tail lately because it's the easiest thing to do. I've been too lazy to put in the barrette that fastens this long mane to my scalp. There was a time where I thought my long hair was very attractive and gave me a snappy edge. Today, I think my long hair has worn out its welcome and I am hankering for a big fat change. But I have to exercise caution here, not be too hasty and put myself in a position I will regret.

The mother I came to love and adore, Evelyn, had a

high-maintenance hairdo. She was a weekly visitor at the local beauty parlor. She also had long hair, which I almost never saw loose. She wore it in a French twist and slept with it that way. The front of her hair was cropped and permed. She had it teased and sprayed and fashioned into a very handsome pompadour type business, which stayed fixed in place till the next shampoo and set. My mother never washed her own hair. Her hairdo was created by professional beauticians.

I, on the other hand, dread the beauty parlor like poison. They snap you into a seriously unbecoming cape and force you to stare at yourself in a mirror while they snip away at your hair and smear stinky coloring on your head. Also, they do a highly unpleasant hair wash where you have to sit stiff on a chair with your head back, practically breaking your neck, while some clumsy fledgling pulls your hair, ostensibly shampooing it. Invariably, I get wet and spend the rest of the time miserable in my shirt.

While Ev was the beauty parlor's best customer, I wouldn't be caught dead there. As I write this, I realize that so much of my behavior is reactive. I want to change that pattern. I need to let go of my stupid, knee-jerk responses to my mother. I must create the self I want to be, irrespective of our similarities and differences. I don't want to condemn myself to look like a disheveled, overgrown teenager just to spite my mom.

I'm a grandma and still trying to get a rise out of my mom. And that's after we became the best mother and daughter team on the planet! That's after years of formal and informal soul-searching on the subject, years of professional training to help everybody else, years of

Twelve Step recovery and just about every imaginable diet ever conceived.

Do I dare allow myself to trust that I'm at the crossroads and am doing the right thing? Could it be that there is a solution and I am finally part of it?

## *April 11th*

Yesterday I finished reading a gruesome book on eating disorders. It was clearly no pleasure to witness that amount of impassioned insanity. I felt it was my duty to read it, being as I am an addiction psychologist as well as a dyed-in-the-wool compulsive overeater. The author was inordinately articulate, with an inspiring ability to self-disclose. She brings you right into her craziness, no holds barred. She vividly portrays the frenzy of her binge and purge cycles.

What she revealed in graphic detail was hard to swallow. I, who have bitten and chewed some ridiculous food excesses, found that her binge descriptions kept ringing my appetite alarm. I am admitting this even though it is terribly embarrassing.

As I raced through her endless stuffing, accompanying her on her journey between the sweet and salty, crunchy and mushy, I got hungry. I read and I salivated. All the while, told myself: "This is nuts. You are reading a book about a person so outrageously ill that she vomited, starved and exercised herself down to a fifty-pound bodyweight. Her book should be another kind of alarm, a warning that a nuclear bomb is coming."

Lunatic that I am, I got the munchies.

I read the book, gobbled it up, devoured it and was

both horrified and morbidly curious to see where it was going. I publicly declare that I raced through the book to get to the part where she gets down to fifty pounds. I was drawn to it like the onlookers at an accident scene who slow the traffic to a crawl just to take a peek. It's human nature—it's him, not me, thank God.

I have never had the misfortune to include anorexia in my bag of eating disorder tricks. I think I secretly envy the control, the absolute willpower that must be exercised. I've always found slim people to look better. I inherited my mother's disdain for fat people and admiration for thin ones.

Anorexics, of course, upset me. I know enough today to feel completely compassionate. This is a vicious sickness, with no enviable features. While being pencil-thin might look gorgeous in clothes, the insanity raging within the psyche is nothing I would trade for in a lifetime.

## April 15th

I went to a funeral two days ago. I had known the woman for twenty years. For over two decades, I had been a sounding-board for her and her extended family.

Over the years, she and I had countless conversations about her daughter, who has some serious issues, including raging bulimia. The mother went to her grave with a huge burden of secrets that might have been too immense for one human being to contain. She was always so solid and sane. She was a rock for her family.

I think, however, that I need to mention that she easily weighed at least three-hundred pounds. In all our years together, she never bemoaned her weight problem or any aspect of it.

There were hundreds of people at this funeral. She was a beloved woman in her community. The fact that she was so enormous was immaterial. Having no self-pity, she evoked no pity.

Undeniably, people saw that she was grossly overweight. Possibly, they talked about her behind her back. But there was something about her, a spirit and personality, that just swept her size out of the picture, leaving space for two souls to communicate.

I've always envied people who can eat, get fat and accept it. I wish I could be in a place in which gaining weight would not be a cause for the public announcement of my shame, sadness and self-loathing. What I mean is, I wish I could bear the consequences like an adult, like she seemed to do.

May her soul rest in peace.

## *April 23rd*

I thought about it yesterday and realized that eating is the most private thing I do. Of course, this is when I'm eating in private! The truth is, I love eating in private. I can chew with my mouth open, I can rub butter on crackers with my fingers. No one is around to admonish me, stare at me in disbelief or just plain find me disgusting.

These moments are none of anyone else's business. They are not intended for public scrutiny. I do not have to be original and brilliant; I don't need to be loving and funny. No, sir. It's a private party and no one else is invited. It is my refuge and sanctuary. It's what I guess you would call my version of chilling out. It's how I relax and calm down.

As I'm saying all of this, I am getting an insight into the secret world, behind closed doors, that people seek in order to play out their ritualistic compulsions. If someone has a secret sexual yearning, it is normally actualized in private, hush-hush. Isn't it strange that my little food forays take on a similar costume to something sexual?

I like to dillydally about in my kitchen, nibbling on this and that. I call it my "caper on the sly." This is when eating is fun. This is that segment of my love affair with food that is the most dangerous, risky business—when I know that a family member can walk into the kitchen or my bedroom and catch me red-handed. This is the epitome of the forbidden fruit department, the heart-pumping thrill of being a bad girl, wondering if I will get caught this time.

Can you imagine? At my age, I'm still afraid I'll get caught, yelled at or humiliated.

If I examine my life, how I conduct myself and think, I have to say that I have virtually no dark corners. I don't have any secret insanities and compulsions. The only arena in which I am even remotely daring and wild is this food thing. I don't have a secret irresistible urge to drink, gamble, stalk someone, check out porn on the internet, or worship the devil. Definitely not. I suppose I've channeled all my dark, libidinal energy into my relationship with food.

It's not as if I feel sexual when I'm eating but, in fact, food does provide sensual pleasure. It appeals to the senses of smell and taste, obviously. I'm in a definite liaison with touching it and putting it in my mouth. Let's not fail to remember that my mouth is a very sensitive area of my body; my lips and tongue are highly engaged while I'm eating. My eyes delight at what's on the plate. The visual experience of setting my sights on the tasty items I'm about to ingest gets me worked up.

I still think about meals or treats with disproportionate lust. If I know I am going somewhere where there might be some snappy food items, I think to myself: "Oh, am I going to have a ball!" Just the thought some sexy desserts has typically had me salivating, chomping at the bit.

Good gracious. It sounds like I am talking about a romantic tryst. All this talk of lust and sexy desserts, yikes… I was never conscious of these connections. I was not aware of my sexuality's role in my food appetite. It never used to come to mind back when I'd wolf down a bunch of very average-to-poor-tasting cookies.

When I think about it, all addicts lust greedily after the objects of their addictions. Irrespective of whether the irresistible urge is actualized in gambling, internet sex or simply food, there is that passionate, urgent spirit of: "Oh, baby, here I come." Now that I am breaking it down, now that I am teasing apart various elements of my relationship with food, I see that eating provides me with certain kinds of emotions I don't otherwise experience in my fairly normal life.

If I am to be perfectly honest with myself, the wild me–the uninhibited me, the risk-all-and-be-dangerous and daring me–only comes out in the plate.

Now I have to go pack for our weekend reunion with Lewis in Amsterdam. I think he will be quite surprised to see how snappy I look. We have theater tickets and an invitation to dine with our good friends, the Divons. Dining with a diplomat serving his country... ho hum! This is a first for all of us.

## *May 3rd*

Somewhere along the line, during the excruciating era called Ellie's Menopause, I had the good fortune to meet Evan. Evan is remarkable. He truly is the consummate psychiatrists' psychiatrist. He plays our sessions like a Stradivarius. It would be thrilling to meet with him forever, if we were only talking about our patients, mine or his, rather than Little Ellie's past or Big Ellie's here and now.

I appreciate the fact that I see him on rare occasions, as he shuttles back and forth between Israel and America. As much as I adore him, I just don't have the energy or interest to undergo therapy of this nature on a regular basis. A large part of me would really rather skip out on the session we have coming up in less than a week.

This does not mean that I have chosen to live out my life semi-comatose; it does not mean that I formally shut the door on my mixed feelings and pain, but it does mean that I no longer choose to wallow in it, feel victimized by it and reduced to helplessness because of it.

Excessive attachment to our "story" cripples us and stifles our growth. We think we must dignify our thoughts, revere them and keep them well-oiled. This is especially true for our traumas. We overdo it, constantly breathing life into our *stories*, never forgetting. We sanctify memories.

I believe that if we don't do enormous spiritual work, if we don't find the tools to recover, we will keep oxygenating our pain. We need to use good sense and judgment. We need to be able to make space for logic to step in and take command when our broken hearts can only drown us.

Now, I am clearly not the little girl of five who woke up in the Bronx with both eyes bandaged, the little girl who could not do anything for herself. I am no longer the girl who was fed, clothed, bathed and soothed by an unknown medical staff–a frightened little girl who was certain she would never see the light of day again.

I am a happily married mother of four, grandmother of more than a dozen. Bermuda was a lifetime ago. How could I still be that little girl?

I am trying every which way to reconnect to the pain and terror she experienced. I want to release myself from her trauma.

At the end of the day, in no uncertain terms, Little Ellie was loved and cherished by her parents. My brother adored me and, as far as I was concerned, he was a god. The fact that no one in the family dynamic knew or was able to bail me out of my mess is not a reason to feel bitterness toward them.

By all accounts, I should have gone nuts. I should have been so gaga by my twenties that I would have either needed serious hospitalization or a cemetery. But I survived. And when I say that, I mean it very seriously. There was a turning point. There was a moment in time where it could have gone either way. God interceded, stepped in and made sure Andy Lynton would bring me to Transcendental Meditation. Since I began, I have never missed a day of morning meditation.

I have been meditating for considerably more than

half of my life. Irrespective of the peaks and valleys I have traversed since making my spiritual vows, I have been on a fairly steady, one-way course toward enlightenment. My progress is reliable and gratifying. It would be foolhardy to flick it off as too significantly distant from perfection to qualify as impressive growth. I will not discredit myself in that way. It would be grossly unjust.

While I am no superstar in the weight-loss marathon, I am an Olympic gold medal winner in the human spirit race.

Although not spiritually perfect yet, I don't consider myself a bad person anymore for feeling angry or insecure. These are not testimonies to failure. Absolutely not; I love being honest with myself. It's a thrilling life and the universe keeps providing me with more challenges. I get them as I can handle them, at the right time and in the right order.

I want to exercise my privilege as a woman of strong heart and mind to make right choices, to ensure that I live well in joy and health, always.

## *May 7<sup>th</sup>*

I spent the first twenty minutes of our obscenely expensive, abbreviated (fifty-minute) hour jumping from one thing to another as if I were free-associating with my beloved psychoanalyst, Sidney. Evan had no trouble following; it was apparent in his eyes. After those twenty minutes of ranting and soliloquizing, I told him what a thrill it is to be with him. It gives me a sense of untold safety. It is a rare gift to be completely contained, understood and accepted simultaneously.

Yet, as I told him, I have no desire to continue piecing together fragments of painful memories, brief scenes and themes that horrify me, make me sad and make me wish I had left enough alone. He replied that such a thing isn't necessary, but I know that's crap. Invariably, when we meet, I rattle off an endless stream of childhood events and humiliations. Something in me wants to be sure that Evan will bear witness to the atrocities. But just as desperately as I want him to know me, I want to avoid this foray into Little Ellie's life.

So here I am, hugely conflicted. It would be easier if Evan resided just around the corner–or maybe that's an illusion. As it is, I must drive for hours, give up precious time, of which I have little lately, and pay a king's ransom to look at, for the millionth time, what makes me tick.

On some level, there is value to being in the presence of someone so well-trained, so thoroughly experienced and human. We have very exciting times in that room. He is unquestionably my intellectual equal. But I have to ask myself, will he be the one? Will he bring me the serenity for which I so deeply yearn?

I think it will be only fair to put off my next visit with Evan for a few months. He so understands, bless him.

## *May 12th*

I woke up yesterday morning determined to keep my points as low as could be so that I would not endanger myself at my sister-in-law's barbecue, scheduled for lunch.

To please her, I dressed like a doll, deliberately wearing slim-fitting pants. I even went to the trouble of accessorizing my outfit with a handsome necklace of sumptuous tiger-eye stones. I caught a lot of compliments. That crowd is used to seeing me in baggy attire, looking *schlumpy* in pinks and purples. This time I decided to play dress-up and throw everybody off. I figured the outfit would match the seriousness of my intent to keep my eating monsters at bay.

It all went pretty well until they started passing around the diet chocolate ice-cream pops, which turned out to be of modest point value. My older son rather delicately suggested I pass up my pop. I took it on the chin and let it go.

Two seconds later, I was doing the dirty deed in the kitchen, gobbling down the pop that was rightfully mine. Talk about a mental case. Talk about a spiteful baby who isn't going to let anyone get the best of her. I was eating that ice-cream so fast, I'm surprised I didn't choke on it.

Just as I was getting close to the stick, a cousin came in to go to the bathroom and innocently inquired as to why I was eating ice cream in the kitchen on the hush-hush. I asked her: "Didn't you hear him tell me I didn't need the ice cream?" She smiled and said: "I never figured you for a person who would do what you're told." I retorted: "You are right. But I didn't want to give anyone a reason to further discuss me or analyze my eating. So I had my cake and ate it too, here in private."

After the first bite, revenge didn't taste so sweet. I wish I were brave enough to have made my point to myself and then thrown out the damn thing. Maybe next time.

## May 15<sup>th</sup>

I had a dream two nights ago that I must relate. I was in some mythical city, yet it felt like Jerusalem. All the doors were closed to me. Things that I knew, that I had initiated, no longer existed. I had somehow become nameless, stripped of my identity. Before me lay a path of thick mud and as I set out upon it, I happened to see my feet. My beautiful green velvet pumps were encased in thick mud. Out of nowhere appeared my husband, who hoisted me up and draped me over one shoulder. We passed skunks with odd yellow markings on their backs. The stench was overpowering, but he plodded on. We passed wild animals. Nothing was a deterrent. I felt such a surge of gratitude.

Before we could escape, I was awakened by the sound of my husband calling my name. He was worried that I was having a nightmare. Apparently, I was moaning in my sleep.

The Chinese herbs I am taking are causing me to create dreams filled with torturous emotions and scenes. Concepts like loss of identity often crop up. Sometimes I will dream about things like communication devices that don't work and I am left unable to get in touch with the world. It's OK that I have these dreams; they present sides of myself to me that invite examination.

## May 19<sup>th</sup>

I am currently exploring my narcissism.

Just saying this about myself is startling. I never talk about this part of me.

I had guests at my house last Friday night, entertained

them magnificently, then decided I'd had enough and excused myself to go take a bath. This was not only rude to my guests but left my husband and others to clean up the mess. On what planet do I live? How could I have been so self-centered? I am so ashamed. I almost always do the dishes.

I can say in my own defense that there are many arenas in my life in which I am phenomenally generous—with my heart and mind, with my compliments and support, with my time and my pocketbook. I am a giver. Unfortunately, I am a lazy doer. Bear with me while I explore this.

Let's face it, my mom was very busy, rarely at home in the daytime, and Olga took care of us. I never in my life saw my mother vacuum or iron. She *was* fastidious and would grow wild if I left a spoon in the sink; naturally, I was not allowed to cook in her kitchen. I would make a big mess and had a bad reputation as a clumsy girl. No one took the time to teach me to coordinate my hands to the task and I grew up virtually incapable of cutting an onion or tomato.

As I am writing this, I feel like weeping. I am a middle-aged woman who is embarrassingly inefficient at the normal physical tasks involved in caring for myself and my home. What the housewife takes for granted is a monumental task to me. When Shoshi is on vacation, I consider myself heroic for keeping the house tidy.

Well, Steps Five through Seven require you to seriously expand your spirituality. The whole deal revolves around spiritual expansion. If you truly let go of your ego—the sky's the limit. But if you make this a purely psychological endeavor and not a spiritual one, you will not get far.

You may put down your addiction, like anyone else whose habit becomes extinct, but you are most likely going to continue to be obsessive about something else. You will not become an exemplary human being. You definitely will not feel it is your moral obligation to help others who still suffer. Most likely, you will be very proud of yourself for overcoming your addiction. But if you are not humble enough, you will have gypped yourself out of a precious opportunity to enlarge your spiritual life.

It is not too late, at least I pray not. I want to shed the lazy, reluctant adult. I want to set aside time in the day for domestic chores. Even though I am slow and clumsy, I will improve over time if I allow myself to do so.

I have no desire to become a good baker; that would be a dangerous and lousy excuse to eat my own cakes and get fat on them. I want to start preparing salads that are handsome and nutritious. I want to make them lovingly, not begrudgingly. I want to make them as a gesture of goodwill toward my home, my family, and myself.

## *May 22nd*

It occurs to me that I have a passion for other people's stories. There is nothing I love more than getting lost in fiction or fact that is not my own. For various reasons, some of which I can surmise, I took an early shine to television. As far back as I can remember, I was glued to the tube. Except for cowboy shows, it was always appealing. In that box, other lives lived for me. As long as I was watching, I basically ceased to exist; my life's pain was eradicated for the moment. As long as I watched the television, fusing myself into others' lives, I had a brief respite from my current reality.

When I discovered the joy of reading, I was yet again taken to another world. What a delight! I could control this; I could start and stop at will, pausing to savor scenes. It was a pleasure entirely different from the television. It allowed me to exercise my imagination and it sensitized me to language. As I grew linguistically, my vistas expanded. I became capable of gobbling on much more sophisticated literary adventures.

The more I read, the more I wanted to write. It was my first creative outlet and I was in heaven.

I cannot remember a time in my life that I wasn't a word-weaver. There's something about my style with words that is elaborate and picturesque. I am fortunate to be an unblocked, fluent speaker and thinker. People love to hear me talk. People love to hear me and the sentences I compose.

My mother was a writer. Bless her soul, she had a way with words I have never witnessed anywhere else. This gift was one of many she generously passed on to me. She took great joy in reading my words.

I fancied myself a writer at a young age. My only problem was that Stephanie, my best friend forever, was also a writer. I kept my literary talents under wraps for years so as not to appear to be in competition with her. Stephanie was the writer and Ellie was the Earth Mother. We held fast to these personae. Even though while she was still alive, I wrote two books and hundreds of poems, papers and articles, Stephanie was the writer of the two of us. Since her untimely passing, I have allowed myself to become The Writer.

Stephanie—oh, how I miss her. She's been on my mind so much lately. Last week, I found a picture of us. It was taken the last time I ever saw her. Who could have imagined that I would never see her again after that, except in the casket that cradled her dead self?

Her disappearance was born of extreme circumstances. She was brutally stabbed by an intruder who left her to bleed to death. I had no way to process this almost three decades ago and still today, I feel I am constitutionally incapable of doing anything with her death and the way it took her over.

It was spring and my kids were still young. I was sitting cross-legged on my bed at 6:20 on a Tuesday morning. All four of my children were sleeping in my room. The boys were my guards and we guarded the girls in kind. Michael was in Istanbul, exploring on his own, laying the groundwork for what promised to be an adventure for both of us. I was due to join him on Thursday.

When the phone rang, I thought it was Michael, figuring he wanted to catch us all in the early morning before we started our day.

I was shocked to hear my father's voice on the other end of the phone. I was in permanent dialogue with America and my rapid mathematical head told me my father was calling well past his bedtime.

"What are you doing up, Pop? It's 11:20 at night there."

"What are you doing, my child?"

"I'm meditating, Daddy, and besides, I asked you first. Why aren't you sleeping?"

"I just got off the phone with Lewis and he told me to call you. I was thinking tonight about the first time I met Leon Bernstein. You know, darling, I met him years before you ever became friends with Stephanie. He is a gentle man."

"Daddy, you are not sleeping because of Stephanie's father? You needed to call Lewis and reminisce about Stephanie's father? What's the matter with you?"

This call was starting to give me the creeps.

"Darling, I'm going to tell you something and then I'm going to hang up the phone. I'm going to go to sleep and you can call me at seven o'clock my time, in eight hours."

I was thinking, with all this build up, that he was about to announce that Leon Bernstein had passed away.

"Darling, Stephanie was murdered, sometime between Sunday night and Monday morning, in Venice beach. The funeral is next Sunday in New York."

I hung up the phone and screamed. My children all woke up. I believe they thought something had happened to Michael. I couldn't tell them Stephanie was murdered. I just said she died. They were shocked and tried to comfort me.

My father's declaration and his choice to curtail the conversation left me literally breathless. I could barely speak. I was stunned. I was frozen.

Robotically, with God knows what forced smile on my face, I fed the kids and sent them off. One hour later, alone in the house, I was in a bizarre state. What do you do when you hear news of this magnitude? What is right? What is wrong? This was the first time someone close to me had died.

I proceeded to make phone calls to California. It was Monday night there and every single, solitary friend of Stephanie's that I called had no idea she was murdered. How absurd—I was calling from Jerusalem to tell everyone that Stephanie was dead and gone. I had no words of consolation for myself; I can't imagine how I commiserated with all of them, some of whom had spoken to her or seen her the day before. I was the messenger, thousands of miles away, telling them about a crime perpetrated right under their noses.

With each call, I became more distant from the event, of which I knew almost nothing. Call after call, I was getting better at my job—bearer of bad news.

When I finished calling her California people, I began making phone calls within Israel. I called my boss at the university to say I was not going to Turkey and would be missing for an extra week, possibly. I had a full roster of family therapy clients I had to cancel. I needed airline tickets and more important than anything, I had to track down Michael, who was somewhere in Istanbul.

It was hard to communicate past a strained language barrier. The hotel receptionist couldn't understand me and I couldn't figure out what he was talking about. All I could gather was that my husband wasn't there. It took hours to find him.

I think I sat on the phone for the entire morning. By the afternoon, two packs of cigarettes later, I was ready to mother my children till I had to leave for the airport. All the kids either knew Stephanie personally or at least knew her pictures and overheard our wonderful phone calls. She was part of our family mythology. She was an epic hero and eternal frame of reference.

By the time I got on that plane, the midnight non-stop to New York, I had successfully, or so it seemed, glued myself together, regained my composure and begun planning the eulogy and what I would wear to the funeral.

I was nowhere near hysterical. I was on automatic pilot, completely oblivious to what I was feeling. I don't remember anything about the plane ride. I know only that I got to New York on Wednesday morning, hopped a cab and went straight to my parents' house.

I was in a kind of trance state. I functioned. Somehow, I managed to be witty and gracious, holding court at Stephanie's parents' house. I was charming and philosophical.

Looking back on this, I see all the earmarks of a total split between my head and my heart. I didn't even realize that I was doing this. I'm sure if someone would have pointed it out, I would have become defensive, saying something like, "I'm a meditator, I am a deeply philosophical person. I am not an emotional *shmateh*. Stephanie is gone. We must move on. It's what she would have wanted from us. Don't accuse me of being cold. I'm the warmest, most loving person you know."

When I got back to Israel after the funeral, I felt compelled, at least intellectually, to deal with Stephanie's death. Even though I was managing so well, I had an inkling that this should have been more devastating than it was. I called my dear friend Nachi, the one who helped me out years before with the bulimia. He invited me to come to his home in Jaffa to participate with him in some kind of adventure that would connect me emotionally to my loss.

We ended up spending three mornings in a row together. Each day I brought gastronomic delights to honor the generosity of time and spirit that Nachi offered. I brought candy, cookies and fruit. I ate almost all of it by myself, nibbling constantly. I clearly wasn't paying any attention to what I was stuffing down my gullet. As long as I could move my right hand back and forth from the plate to my mouth, I was safe.

Even though I had an extraordinary time in Jaffa, I see now that very little we did put me in touch with the unthinkable–death by stabbing. Death by her own kosher meat knife. Death by the slow bleeding out of her vital organs. According to the forensic report, it took some minutes for her to die.

How could I possibly deal with this? Make sense of it? Visualize it and still maintain my sanity? I chose to keep it a linguistic event. I could construct grammatical sentences about it, talk about it, but I could not possibly even begin to grasp what I was feeling.

I was lucky, as I was used to being worlds apart from her. This was just another version of it.

Last week, staring at our picture, at our last time together, I began to wonder about myself and why it is that when things become gruesome, I can automatically tell myself: "I cannot afford the luxury of falling apart." It was my father's mantra. I have carried it with me for years.

By not becoming hysterical, by staying philosophical, I manage to fool myself into believing that I am on top of things.

Eva and Shoshi can literally cry all day when they need to; their heartache is palpable. I would hate to spend the day in tears. The idea repels me. I can cry, but I prefer to keep far away from convulsive sobs. I am too ADHD to stay focused on my own pain.

I cry for my patients. Their stories touch me. My own are better experienced at a distance. At least this is how I have conducted my emotional business so far.

But now things are taking a different shape. The jig is almost up because I am weaning myself off my use of food and TV as an escape hatch. I am becoming braver and more honest. Gradually, I am facing my pain and not denying it. In time, my head, my heart and my body will reunite in precious harmony.

By becoming a psychologist, I placed myself squarely in the middle of other people's lives. As opposed to my pals on TV and novels, I now had real life dramas to attend to. The rigors of failed existence were my daily challenge.

It's OK with me that my escape involves other people's lives. It takes some of the burden off my shoulders for a while. I get a brief respite, a breather and even a chance to do some good in the world.

## *June 7$^{th}$*

I just called to wish my beloved daughter Miriam Malka a happy anniversary. In so doing, I began reliving that moment in time years ago. What a wedding! What an unforgettable event. The bride and the groom were glorious. I have never attended another wedding so honestly spiritual.

But if I'm being honest about my struggles to rise above little Ellie Belly, I have to reflect sincerely on those days leading up to the wedding.

Hila, my beloved acupuncturist and Chinese herbalist, came to my home for a session. I lay with the needles for close to an hour. Call me crazy, but I think it was unwise to stay stuck for so long. Several hours after the treatment, I was feeling unglued and nervous. My moods were bobbing up and down and I felt dangerously close to the edge. I wanted no part of this. I called Hila and told her my theory about the duration of the treatment. She clearly stated she did not think that was the problem. She advised me to start my new herbal remedies as soon as possible.

When I picked up my herbs the next day, Sara–the herbalist who runs the pharmacy–told me: "Dr. Katz, you sure are something. We've never had a client as patient as you. For almost a year and a half now, you have taken over fifteen different remedies, none of which have delivered the hoped-for goods. You suffer more from side effects than you do from benefits. It's amazing how you don't give up."

I left her place thinking that I was just handed a supreme compliment. What a wonderfully loyal person I was. I stuck with Hila, whom I absolutely adored, in the hopes that together she and I would bring me to harmony. But maybe my loyalty was foolhardy…

Unfortunately, the herbs *really* jammed me up that time and I became nervous and crabby. I kept telling myself that I just needed to ride it out and that the herbs would eventually do me good.

By Saturday, the night before the wedding, I was a complete wreck. Toward the evening, I sat on my bed with my husband. He patted me gently as I rattled off a list of all the different ways in which I was feeling bad. He reads me like a book and is well aware of how my moods swing–that they go as easily as they come.

Obviously, I was worked up and it wasn't just the herbs.

"Silly," I thought, "how could you be such a self-absorbed maniac, getting pats from Michael when you should be patting 'the best of the big girls' on the night before her wedding?

"You are using the excuse that the herbs are messing up your mind. The truth is, I suppose, you are very excited about the wedding tomorrow night and you don't know what to do with these emotions. How typical! It seems all you're good for is to stay frozen in this bed, ducking out of the wedding preparations. Funny you're not eating like a nutcase."

Just as I was about to plunge into serious hibernation, my friend Ruthie rang the bell. She came all the way from California to be at this event. She has known the future bride since that daughter of mine took up residence in my belly.

Ruthie is the most enthusiastic person I know. She also never takes things lightly; I mean this as a compliment. She was not about to let me get too casual or immobile and weasel out of my motherly duties. In her special way, she let me know that I would pay a heavy price in conscience if I didn't race to my daughter's arms to be at her beck and call. My beloved Ruthie had come from spending hours fluttering around my daughter in my stead. Now it was time for me to envelop my daughter with blessings.

I jumped in the car, rushing to the precious bride-to-be,

who was staying a couple of blocks away from me with her wedding entourage. She was exuberant. It's her nature; we are twins in that way. She had a palpable, unmistakable glow of serenity about her. It was disarming and I was grateful for the respite from my tensions.

This gal is a deeply philosophical person who from the beginning took the idea of holy matrimony to a very serious place. For her, it was to be a blessed ceremony, opening the gates to a future with a man who still seems to be her perfect completion. According to the Orthodox tradition, these two had yet to even hold hands. They knew each other well, though, through long heart-to-hearts. This is their adopted style, born of knowing a more modern life and choosing piety.

She was waiting for me to join her for the ritual purification, a plunge into a special pool of water called a *mikveh*. For weeks we had been talking about this. We were scheduled to leave in a few hours and she could see from my demeanor that something was amiss. I guess I brought some vestiges of self-involvement with me. I forgot to leave them at home.

I started to go into my song and dance about how I didn't want to go to bed late, how I wasn't a suitable candidate for the festivities: "Darling, I am decidedly secular in my Judaism; I've never been to the *mikveh*."

Who was I selling this nonsense to?

This little angel, this highly enlightened teacher of a daughter, just looked at me and said: "It's alright, Mama. I know my lifestyle is somewhat incomprehensible to you. That's okay. Truly. It will not affect our relationship."

Now, I was hearing this, but it wasn't getting through

to me because I was so deep in my own mess. I couldn't absorb the truth at that moment.

In came my daughter's sister-in-law-to-be, who said: "Ellie, no way are you not coming." But you know what? I was still convinced that all I needed was to be left alone.

Things started to steam up when I rattled off again my list of all the reasons why I was not going to the *mikveh*. Ruthie pulled me off to the side so that no one would hear us. It was clear to her that my only way of coping was to head for inactivity with a passion. I guess my body language announced a ferocious stubbornness that made me deaf to all her pleas. I was getting more and more aggravated. I hated the pressure. I hate getting weaseled into doing things I don't want to do. I was prepared to spend a pathetic evening in bed with food and TV instead of making the stretch for my daughter's sake.

"Ellie, your daughter is getting married in less than twenty-four hours and she wants her mother to partake of a very important experience. Are you following me?"

All of a sudden I understood that my infantile, self-destructive desire to escape was just that: infantile and self-destructive. Here the universe was not only offering me a huge look in the mirror, but also a glorious opportunity to know purification. I made an about-face, stood up and said: "Let's go."

During the ride, I was deep in thought: "I am so proud of myself for putting her before me. I surely need to do that more often. Why don't I like to stretch my limitations? I need to change all that. I need to take myself out of the center of all this. Right now, the bride is more important than the mother of the bride, who needs her admittedly creepy little comforts. Right now, the bride has invited me to share in one of the biggest moments in her life and I'm doing it for her because she deserves this from her mother."

I had never been to a *mikveh*, but perhaps it was time for me to entertain the idea of a serious dip in holy water. I wanted the water to rinse away years of laziness and craziness. In the end, after the baptism, maybe I would be more spiritually evolved.

The attendant at this bathhouse was gentle and discreet. I swear I was surrounded by angels. Each time I plunged into the waters, the attendant's little voice said: "*Ka-sher.*" I cannot imagine how to convey what hearing this stamp of approval sounded like. It could have been so otherwise; it could have been just automatic, meaningless and superficial. But it was so pure and so reassuring. It was as if the attendant knew my heart and knew that I was using her waters for a baptism and not as a readying to rejoin my husband in the marriage bed, as women must do in Orthodox families.

I tried to use these holy waters to liberate myself from all that was imperfect in me. When I came out of my final dip and the sweet little angel of an attendant helped me into my robe, I began to wail. I don't remember crying like that in years. It came from a place deep inside. It was a wail of pain and hope.

I was in awe of what had transpired. I felt so close to the bride, my sweetheart daughter who was about to cross the threshold into holy matrimony. That's an expression I've heard for years, "holy matrimony." In this specific case, being with her before and during her wedding, I can testify with no reservation that her wedding ceremony was an indisputable act of holiness. I was a witness and it was a privilege.

I haven't been in a *mikveh* since. I've had no occasion to do so. It was a moment frozen in time—one I will always cherish.

## June 19*th*

Today is a special day because my eldest son is doing celestial justice to Gershwin and Chopin in the other room. He is playing the piano my parents bought when I was five in the hope that my brother Lewis and/or I would reveal some incredible hidden talents.

I don't recall Lewis ever playing the piano. He hobbled along on the trumpet, briefly. But he has a great ear and a deep appreciation of all things musical. I am a singer, always have been. My skills on the pianoforte were third-rate, so I didn't overinvest myself in them. Although I must say that when I moved to Israel, I took piano lessons twice weekly for almost eight years. I loved the lessons and I loved practicing. But there's no way I could describe myself as any kind of piano talent.

My eldest child is talented and makes me faint with his piano playing. Who would ever have thought that this kid would have the talent and wherewithal to put in tireless hours and love every minute of it? When he's out there turning the piano of my childhood into the instrument of angels, I feel like my office is in Carnegie Hall. I have to use all my restraint to keep from jumping up from my chair and stealing a smooch. What a joy.

## June 21$^{st}$

Today is the first day of summer. Although I still have three more months until this experiment ends, I cannot help but take stock. Where am I with the goals I proposed for myself exactly one year ago?

Yes, I have lost weight. Yes, I have attended Weight Watchers faithfully, sort of. I am still Twelve-Stepping through my life as deliberately as possible, speaking with Helen on a daily basis. On top of all that, I have begun to exercise in a serious way.

On a more important note, I have scoured my soul, making serious renovations in my psyche. In short, I have made peace with the beast that I fed and groomed. I have even beckoned it to kindly take its leave.

But I'm not finished with the renovations yet.

Maybe because I am actively putting food in its place these days, emotions I ignored are cropping up. An uninvited guest just snuck its way into my head. Thoughts of me and my mom duking it out are crowding my consciousness.

"Now is the time to explore the mother-daughter issues bravely," I tell myself. "You are evolved enough to do this without having to resort to food to numb your emotions."

I listen to my own inner guide and start to heed the call to make sense of my past.

My parents did the best they could to soften the blows of my traumas. This might sound absurd, as these events were never spoken about–truly, never, ever–until I asked about them; but I cannot fault them for any of it, for my eye surgery or for my rapid growth spurt. What happened in Bermuda was clearly not their doing.

My mother didn't help me cope with the events that scared me to death; they probably scared her to death too! She was unavailable emotionally to help me sort through my pain and shame. Maybe it was too spooky for her. Maybe she had no way to deal with it and hoped I would just move on and forget it.

The fact that it escalated my already-established eating disorder isn't too hard to fathom psychologically. My mind split me off from what I going through. I blacked it out. As long as I had food and my thumb attached to my hand, I could live.

I didn't even remember the eye surgery until I was twenty, at Sidney's. The Bermuda travesty came up in my thirties. I'd call that heavy amnesia.

This year, I have already started to look at this in a different way, but my understanding is too partial. I need to investigate further.

## *June 28<sup>th</sup>*

I decided yesterday that I needed to talk to Evan after all. We had a forty-five-minute long distance chat and I told him some of my latest insights about eating. I explained that I originally saw it as an act of warfare against my mother; my reaction to my traumas was to seek comfort through my hands and get back at her through them as well. Now, however, I have begun to recognize that she was a victim of a society that opted to sweep things under the rug.

Evan and I began to explore various subtle expressions of aggression that I have successfully denied and repressed. I never knew how angry and resentful I can be! I had absolutely no idea that I was anything but sweet and kind. There are lots of sides to me, but I never would have thought that angry was one of them. Through my work on myself, I have come to face sides of myself that I previously kept far from my consciousness.

I had denied my resentment. I had completely buried my anger and fury. No one ever saw it, especially me. That, of course, was due to the way in which food acts on my nervous system. Eating the way I always have has kept me cheerful when I needed to be and numb when I needed to be. I had this down to a science. I could annihilate my feelings through snacks and television. I was actually set-up and completely comfortable as long as I had my trusty remote control and a well-stocked larder.

I am too much of a people-pleaser to lunge for the jugular in an overt way. I have my sneaky little tactics; they mostly inhabit my thoughts. My little musings to myself can seethe with criticism and intolerance. It seems it is to this realm that I have shoved my aggressive side.

Today, I choose to own every piece of myself. If I have a stinky side, I want to take responsibility for creating it and nurturing it. I also hereby give myself permission to let go of it. With Evan's help, with God's help, with Isella's help and, of course, my blessed cooperation, I just might join the club of the ones who move up the ladder towards spiritual enlightenment.

For the next week and a half I will be taking a road trip with my husband, visiting friends along the way. I hope that I will be able to eat the kinds of foods that will only do me good and not tempt me into confusion.

## *July 12th*

It's been almost two weeks since I've written. Michael and I had an absolutely wonderful holiday. It's always a joy to travel with my husband–I love to see the world through his eyes.

The countryside is just what I need from a vacation. The highlight of the trip was a sunset drive through unending green pastures that were peopled with goats. I discovered new meaning in *picturesque*. I felt as if I were part of the panorama. It was paradise.

While we were away, we vowed to limit our internet activities in order to stay in the moment and not be sidetracked by the news. I didn't even realize how peaceful our respite was until it was over; I think I must have become numb to the daily barrage of images, only to be shocked upon our return home. Refugees, beheadings, rapes, and the general global disaster–I have been brought rudely back to this thing we call reality.

Years ago, my anxiety was personal with every hint of escalating conflict in the Middle East. My oldest son was an army officer who grew into an idealistic peacemaker. Once his service was complete, he would have agreed to sit in military jail rather than serve in a combat capacity had the reserves called him up. My other son was part of a rescue/medical team in the air force. One of my biggest fears was that they would somehow meet up together on the battlefield. Thank God it never happened.

It was a pleasure not to turn on a television once while on the road. We spared ourselves from reality. But now that we're back to LIFE, I feel that it's irresponsible to be oblivious to the world at large.

## July 16$^{th}$

I had a visit today from one of my former patients. When last we met, a year ago, she had successfully lost about sixty pounds. That weight loss was dramatic on her. She went from a mountainous-looking gal to a lithe and delicate creature.

Unfortunately, her mania has reared its ugly head again and taken her to very insane places. Her appetite flares up with the mania and in four months she has managed to gain seventy pounds. She still has a certain beauty and charm but her clothes today were ill-fitting and all her monkeying around with the slit in her skirt didn't help matters.

Oddly, she couldn't stop raving about my weight loss. I tried to play it down so as to not make her feel, God forbid, that I was successful and she was a hopeless failure. I tried to seem blasé but she kept raving about how good I look.

What a ridiculous irony. I am so dedicated to the success of my transformation, yet I didn't dare share it. I could still smell plenty of madness on her, so I wanted to keep my personal achievements to myself. Hours later, I still feel sad about the state she's in. It was shocking to see her so transformed. There's a lesson in here somewhere. We are all so frail and on the brink.

## July 20$^{th}$

I feel an urgency to write while the taste of hazelnuts, chocolate chips and cookie dough still lingers in my mouth. I am experiencing a change in my breathing and heart rate, a sense of impending euphoria. But after the elation, sated to the point of nausea, I know there will be the inevitable tumble. Tumble and drop are euphemisms for the plummet, the death-defying dive from the high board into a little bucket of water: in other words, defeat.

I have done it again. I have murdered myself in cold blood. I have turned into a raging bull. Nothing is safe in my path. After the rampage, I have become intensely fragile.

I was sure I was finished with this nonsense by now. For such a long time, I've been meticulous with my food and my honesty. I thought I was learning to deal with my emotions and then I go and do a thing like this.

I know how it happened, of course. Somehow, I ended up the victim of a ferocious political diatribe from my son the pacifist. We then each retreated to our corners. I went to my bedroom; he went to pick up his son from nursery school.

I am largely sympathetic to my son's peaceful inclinations, so it's hard to say where we went wrong. All forms of hatred sadden me. I am repelled by violence and brutality. I have never truly understood the "us/them" identification and I don't know how to handle people who interact with the world in that way. I can't even articulate what the source of our disagreement was.

After he left, I turned on the news and just the sound of the anchor's voice triggered such an exaggerated barrage of existential angst. It was a piece on human trafficking, followed by another failed attempt by refugees to get to Europe by water. They are still counting the drowned.

I said to myself: "Life is an irreparable cesspool. What does it matter if I eat cookies?"

I've been unsettled since we got back from our vacation and I suppose this was about as much as I could take after my brief escape to paradise.

But what comes next?

## *July 22nd*

I have spent the last two days forgiving myself for that insane cookie lapse. It's hard for me to ascertain just what I was up to. I think I used my *weltschmerz*, world pain, as an excuse to lose it and engage in a highly unwarranted, temporary fit of insanity. I am human, after all.

In these last years in OA I have learned that I am powerless when it comes to food. But as my understanding of addiction widens, I have come to learn that I am powerless over the universe. I am not actually even running my own show.

Part of Step Two is finding a way to believe that a power greater than yourself can set things right.

Some people have a hard time believing in this power and its accessibility. Even for those of us who have some kind of God concept, it isn't always clear how to get in touch with it. We don't know the key.

Is worthiness the key? Is ritual the key? Is becoming devoutly religious going to help? These questions will inevitably arise.

I don't know. I never did find out the rules of the game.

How the universe works is unfathomable to me. Faith is not about what I can understand. There is order to this life. Something is in charge of the smooth flow of nature as well as the storms. I dictate neither life nor death.

Without becoming obnoxiously philosophical and off the track, I know that I am helpless in the face of the universe's plans. While it might appear that I am making the choices that shape my life, it's not exactly up to me. One makes plans, but they don't necessarily come to fruition.

"Circumstances beyond our control" is a very descriptive phrase that explains a lot.

There are many things I wish would cease to exist: armies and weaponry, violence and evil, sadness and sickness. Since I am not running the show, I have been training myself to accept what I cannot change–the agony and the atrocity.

Step Three is where you make a well-formed, intellectual and spiritual decision to turn your will and your life over to the care of God as you understand Him: "I can't, God can. I think I'll let God." There's a lot of talk about "turning it over." You simply say: "God, help me."

For some lucky people, consciousness comes sweetly after years of personal struggle. It comes in answer to life lived in self-destructive craziness or glaring immorality.

In my case, unfortunately, it comes and goes like a loose wire connection. It is not entirely sreliable. When I clear a space for it, it is always there. When I'm more in the mood for cookies than God, I pretend He doesn't exist.

When I become overinvested in Ellie, I very conveniently shut God out. In order to let Him back in again, I have to reduce some of the space I am taking up. Here I need a large dose of humility.

Choosing to walk on the path of God, however I conceive of Him, makes me feel better. I feel supported and protected, no longer overwhelmed by life. The illusion that I am in command vanishes. Tiny miracles dot my path and I feel safe inside my own head.

I sometimes dream up little friendly angelic helpers, too. It doesn't matter, as long as I know I am not alone. Something is running this show and it's sure as hell not me.

Sometimes I need to remember that I am an ordinary citizen, without much influence on international conflicts. I go about my business, caring for my family and my patients. I keep up my writing as well as other pleasures. In my own small way, I endeavor daily to make the world a better place with my gifts.

On this date a good number of years ago, I had the privilege of attending a mind/body workshop with some of the most interesting psychiatrists and mental health professionals in the world. We congregated in a mountain hotel ten minutes from my home. The work, which focused on the destructive nature of stress, was steeped in science and medical evidence.

There was a great emphasis on "self-care." We learned how to deal with our own anxieties. About one hundred and thirty people participated–Jews, Moslems and Christians. Love and sanity dominated the scene. Our teachers and facilitators were people on the path, not just theoreticians. It was a tender week, brimming over with goodwill. I was surprised at how well-organized it was.

Now here I sit, dictating my brains out to Shani–my beloved eagle-eye of an assistant, whose very presence in my life is precisely what I need–while a group of birds is playing tag between the lemon trees and rose bushes. My belly is full of legal *noshes*–thank G-d I returned to my senses–the ceiling fan is providing a perfect temperate zone and all is right in my miniscule existence.

There is nothing more productive for me to do until someone in the state department or foreign ministry hears about me and decides to send a limo to pick me up for talks behind closed doors. Wouldn't that be something?

What a delusion of grandeur. It's kind of thrilling to entertain such a fantasy. Believe me, I know I could tell world leaders a thing or two about kindness and tolerance.

## *August 3rd*

On my way here this morning, I had a brief encounter with my husband in his studio. He was busy welding a spectacular metal gate. I wanted so much to hug him and rip open the snaps of his work smock. We both laughed, because he wanted to give me the same big hug but the time wasn't right, so we hugged verbally, with our words and smiles. He said to me: "I don't know if you feel like this, but I love you so much I could die this moment and know I am blessed." I answered: "It's the same for me. I am dumbfounded by these emotions. To love this richly for forty years is nothing short of the miraculous."

This guy has loved me fat, loved me thin and has always made me feel like the greatest gift he could ever imagine. We adore being together, celebrate each other's independence and foster our best selves. I named him Lucky the first week we met, but I always knew which one of us actually lucked out. He is and will always be my proof of a higher power.

It's OK if your higher power is the wind or the ocean—two forces greater than yourself. You can believe that nature has the power to lift your disease and toss it to wind or sea. If you need to, give God a long white beard and glasses. Jazz Him up like a gospel singer. God is so great; He probably would never be insulted by what you do in order to conceptualize Him.

To people who resist this, who find it an affront to

their intellects, I can only offer personal experience. I was harshly critical and intolerant of bargaining with God. I was nauseated by con artists striking deals with the Almighty. I had to get past this. People's transactions with the divine are not my business.

To the dubious and cynical, if you've ever had your heart melt at the sight of a puppy or a majestic sunset, connect to that feeling. It has nothing to do with the intellect.

## *August 10<sup>th</sup>*

I did a Buddhist practice this morning with Debbie during yoga. *Tonglen* is performed in this manner: I visualize someone else's pain and suffering and attempt to internalize it, no matter how gruesome and black. Within me it becomes purified and I send back relief. Today, I envisioned the pain of the multitudes coping with poverty, sickness, war and loneliness. It felt like a small and valuable gesture to the universe.

While I was at it, I forgave myself for celebrating my life while others have challenges impossible to fathom, let alone bear. I gave myself permission to care about the books I write and the things I swallow. I have no choice but to fulfill the commandment to live my life well and help as many people as I can. This is my calling and I do not shirk my duties. I do not believe God would have it any other way. Besides, when God has another plan for me, He'll let me know.

## *August 21<sup>st</sup>*

I have a confession to make: Hear ye, hear ye, I'm about to town cry on myself. Six days ago, my beloved sister-in-law

Tova turned me on to creamy diet ice coffee shakes. I ordered it at her suggestion when we were on a lunch date; when it arrived, I slurped down that tall, frosty cup of crushed ice, decaf, artificial sweetener and skim milk. Four points in all. It was like getting away with murder! I felt like I had pulled off the heist of the century.

A week later, I'm forbidding myself to drink this wild concoction ever again. Professional obligations have kept me away from Weight Watchers lately, but I really am vigilant about my points even when on my own.

It's true that the thick, dreamy arrangement satisfies me on innumerable levels. First of all, it's as close to ice cream as it gets. Coffee ice cream has been a passion of mine since high school, when I would have food orgies with my girlfriend Corky that invariably included Schrafft's by the gallon. What insanity. What shameless disrespect for consequence.

Corky had this fabulous figure. No one in her house had an eating disorder; at least, no one looked like it. That was in the old days when the only problem with food was looking like you loved it too much and couldn't control yourself.

Her family loved to eat and never thought that food was either illicit or dangerous. Corky's mother stocked cookies, cakes and ice cream by the gallon, not the pint. This was so radical for me. It was an unheard of event. In my house, food was the enemy.

At Corky's, I developed a special hankering for coffee-flavored ice cream. My hankering has been shadowing me since then. Luckily, I mostly avoid it. That is, I *did*, until I got wind of the diet ice coffee shake.

After the first sip, I was a goner. By the next day, I was scheming about how I could get to the specific mall where they sell it. I am not a mall moll. I hate shopping and do not frequent garish, tasteless shopping arcades anywhere in the world. But the only place they sell this drink forced me to look for parking and brave the crowds.

By day three, I allowed myself to buy two drinks in one go—one for now and one for later. By day six, I have realized that I cannot go on with this charade and I've decided to stop cold turkey.

Why, you must be asking, am I making such a big stink about a totally benign substance? For one thing, it was ruling my behavior and I don't want something like that to be my master. The whole affair smacked to high heaven of addiction. I'd rather stop before it gets out of hand.

Even worse, I persisted in drinking the diet ice coffee shakes despite the fact that this brew is lethal to my gastrointestinal system. Within forty minutes of ingestion, I get a stomach cramp from hell and spend the next twelve hours coping as my body registers its objections in foul terms. Every day, I've told myself: "Drink this stuff and let's see what happens. Maybe you'll get used to it. Maybe you'll build up a tolerance."

This is addictive thinking. I want That Drink; I don't want to have to give it up. But the truth is, I am not allowed to treat my gut so ruthlessly. Thank God I don't normally react this way to food. But if the universe steps in to this level, I have to pay heed.

La di da, I just recently cut out diet chewing gum too; it was giving me jaw pains. I had never made the connection before and when I did, I knew we had to part company.

## *September 3rd*

I have Weight Watchers in two more days. It will be a month since my last appearance; that's a long time to be away from my relationship with the group and the scale. To tell the truth, I have big plans for this month. I am eager and passionate about seeing lower and lower numbers on that record. I fantasize about Ziv's genuine delight when we see I've lost an almost unimaginable eight pounds in a month. It's what I want; it's what I yearn for. It's possible to do. In fifty-three more hours, I will know just how much success is mine.

## *September 6th*

Holy moly, I really did lose another eight pounds this month! Ziv had tears in her eyes when she weighed me.

September 20th is right around the corner and I have lost thirty-five pounds out of the fifty-pound goal I set for myself at the start of this experiment.

I was waiting for a miracle, I suppose. I was yearning to wake up and change my entire being, my inside as well as my appearance.

I am accepting my only partial headway quite graciously. I feel spiritually generous with myself and particularly tolerant. Over the course of these months, I have been on a truly important journey toward honesty and spiritual refinement. I needed to nourish my healthy self and not the wounded little girl.

I have absolutely not given up hope. I love that about myself. I always believe change is possible.

At Weight Watchers, I felt I owed it to the group to

stand up and tell them an inspiring tale of how I "did it." I shared my saga with the room and told them how I defeated my worst enemy. This necessitated more than weight loss.

I think the crux of the matter is this: When you are your own worst enemy, you have a dangerous and formidable foe. It is I, just I, who louses things up for myself time and again. In every other matter in my life, I am so responsible, so reliable, so sane and efficient. With food, I have historically been a blustering idiot, mentally challenged and spiritually downtrodden.

This year was a real test of bravery. I had to muster my courage and agree to put food in second place. I allowed hidden truths to expose themselves. I dared to confront my weaknesses without heading for the hills.

I think it's a very interesting name for an organization—Weight Watchers. I feel more like a Wait Watcher. It's a study in patience. I sense that I have some more waiting to do before I get all my internal nonsense straightened out.

But who am I kidding? When has anyone ever successfully straightened out *all* their nonsense? It may be the work of many lifetimes.

Ah. Now that is something to which I can look forward.

# At the End of the Day

Well, we've come to the end of my experiment. My twenty-third birthday in OA is coming up in November. I haven't missed a meeting in Jerusalem on a Friday morning yet, not including trips abroad. Helen is still my beloved sponsor whose program message and way of being inspire me.

Miracle of miracles, my precious brother Lewis has found the love of his life. I have been waiting fifty years for him to find a suitable wife, one who will inspire him to discover his true nature and purpose. I have some investment in this deal; I need a sister-in-law I can adore and respect. We had the privilege of meeting his new other half and she is a well-deserved gift.

I don't want to embarrass the hell out of Shani, but the truth is, she has been my right hand–and my left as well–for the writing of this book. I have a built-in editor who keeps me honest and smart. If it weren't for the *noshes* she doles out, I'd be dictating from my La-Z-Boy from a feeling of deprivation. She is the keeper of the salted almonds and thin-sliced yellow cheese. In the beginning of the relationship, I knew I was crazy about her; she never raised an eyebrow when I asked if she wouldn't mind if I snapped bubble wrap while I dictated. For years now, I have been looking for the perfect assistant. I hope I don't give myself the whammy by extolling her virtues in writing.

Michael and I are gearing up for our forty-first anniversary. Last night before bed, he said, "Are you sure it's forty-one and not forty?" I laughed. I'm the family historian; friends swear I have a steel-trap memory.

"Darling," I told Michael, "this is definitely something I remember." I dug up an old photograph of my brother and Michael on our wedding day. They both had long hair. I love the picture. They look so beautiful and so happy.

Michael and I reminisce any number of times a day about our years together, about how much *naches* we have from our four, happily-married children. They have given us untold hours of joy. We're now at the over-a-dozen mark of grandchildren, most of whom we see every week. Our children exhibit generosity of spirit by letting us share in their lives. We both play very active roles in bringing up these kiddies.

I sometimes tell Michael in jest that if his demise precedes mine, I will march into the house and wolf down the entire contents of my alternative medicine cabinet in protest.

Then, if I truly knew I was dying, if I was on a one-way journey to imminent death, would I take back my cigarettes, Diet Cola, daytime TV and cookies? Would I start drinking margaritas and frozen banana daiquiris? You bet!

That's what I say when I'm being cute. The truth is, I

haven't written my bucket list yet. I have been alive long enough to know that there isn't anything out there that I need to complete myself as a human being. I suppose if I knew the Grim Reaper was about to knock at my door, I would just say the *Shma* prayer: "Hear O Israel! The Lord our God, the Lord is one."

I have been savoring the fruits of this year's giant personal transformation. I don't feel the same, I don't look the same. While people admire my substantial weight loss, what they probably don't know is I don't care so much about it anymore.

Yes, it's nice to look better and it's nice to be praised for my courage in excluding so many of the foods most people wolf down for recreation. But for me, the big victory is of an entirely different nature. It's not about being or not being a fat girl. It's about not being a girl anymore.

Hell, I've got fourteen grandchildren. I'm turning sixty-eight this year. Who am I calling a girl?